The Moulin Rouge and Black Rights in Las Vegas

Also by Earnest N. Bracey

Daniel "Chappie" James: The First African American Four Star General (McFarland, 2003)

The Moulin Rouge and Black Rights in Las Vegas

A History of the First Racially Integrated Hotel-Casino

EARNEST N. BRACEY

McFarland & Company, Inc., Publishers
Jefferson, North Carolina, and London

LIBRARY OF CONGRESS CATALOGUING-IN-PUBLICATION DATA

Bracey, Earnest N.
The Moulin Rouge and Black rights in Las Vegas : a history of the first racially integrated hotel-casino / Earnest N. Bracey.
p. cm.
Includes bibliographical references and index.

ISBN 978-0-7864-3992-8
softcover : 50# alkaline paper ♾

1. Moulin Rouge (Hotel-Casino : Las Vegas, Nev.)
2. Hotels — Nevada — Las Vegas — History. 3. Casinos — Nevada — Las Vegas — History. 4. United States — Race relations. I. Title.
TX941.M69B73 2009
647.9409793'135 — dc22 2008045972

British Library cataloguing data are available

On the cover: Cancan dancers at the Moulin Rouge, 1955 (Nevada State Museum and Historical Society, Las Vegas); cards and tabletop ©2008 Shutterstock.

Manufactured in the United States of America

McFarland & Company, Inc., Publishers
Box 611, Jefferson, North Carolina 28640
www.mcfarlandpub.com

To my brother,
James Milton Bracey

Acknowledgments

Some of my colleagues at the College of Southern Nevada suggested, after the publication of my article "The Moulin Rouge Mystique: Blacks and Equal Rights in Las Vegas" in the *Nevada Historical Society Quarterly* in 1996, that I write the full story of the Moulin Rouge hotel and casino. It has been a long and laborious task — that is, to write this important history, while teaching American politics and black American history full-time, especially gathering the scholarly research. But it was, nevertheless, a pleasurable experience. To date, and as far as I know, this book is the most comprehensive work on the historic Moulin Rouge hotel and casino.

I would like to thank Dave Millman of the Nevada State Museum and Historical Society in Las Vegas for providing some of the excellent photographs used in this book, which I know was a serious inconvenience. The Nevada State Museum was undertaking a major relocation to the Springs Preserve, mainly because it had long outgrown its old site located at 333 South Valley View Boulevard. I would also like to acknowledge Lee Brumbaugh, curator of photography at the Nevada Historical Society in Reno, Nevada, for his helpful hints about locating several photographs of the Moulin Rouge when it was first built.

Much appreciation is also due to Sarann Knight-Preddy for her encouragement and moral support. When I first started this endeavor ten years ago, Sarann Knight-Preddy was very kind to me. She gave of her time, memory, and friendship, and I will always be grateful. I am also grateful to her for the material, information and documents she gave me to complete this work. Additionally, she allowed me to interview her at the offices of the Moulin Rouge in 1996, before she finally and sadly gave up on the historic place, after working herself almost into the ground. I had several enlightening and stimulating discussions with her about blacks in Nevada, the city of Las Vegas, and the Moulin Rouge in particular. I am deeply in debt to and my heartfelt and sincere thanks go to Sarann Knight-Preddy; I am also sorry that things, ultimately, did not work out for her and her gifted family members, who worked so hard to make the Moulin Rouge a place to be reckoned with. There is no doubt in my mind that this book is better because of Sarann Knight-Preddy's support and consideration.

I originally wanted to write a follow-up to my 1996 article, but the scope of the material proved to be too massive and too convoluted to be contained in an article. I would also like to give special acknowledgment to the late Nevada historian Gary E. Elliott, who gave me a lot of sound advice when I was a young scholar, just starting out full-time in academia after a twenty-year military career. In addition, I would like to acknowledge professors Alan Balboni and Michael S. Green for their encouraging me to complete this work. Both of these outstanding scholars allowed me to discuss, argue, and explore ideas about the complex nature and difficult history of blacks in Las Vegas with them.

They and other brilliant colleagues at the College of Southern Nevada were excellent sounding boards for this controversial book. I had many discussions with Michael S. Green, who is the editor in chief of the *Nevada Historical Society Quarterly*, about the various nuances and approaches that I should take in bringing this book to fruition. This historical iteration, however, is mine alone. I am also totally responsible for any errors and all of the analysis and interpretations in this first history of the revered Moulin Rouge hotel and casino in Las Vegas.

I am also grateful for the magnificent libraries at the University of Las Vegas, Nevada, and the College of Southern Nevada, and the wonderful librarians, who worked so diligently in helping me track down several obscure works and other hard to find material.

Lastly, I want to thank my wife, Atsuko, for her unstinting and insightful support and advice, as always. Atsuko continues to be helpful in many ways, and this book could never have been written without her.

Contents

Contents

Preface

When I first decided to visit the famous Moulin Rouge hotel and casino again in the summer of 2004 after a fire had gutted the main casino building, I felt an overwhelming sadness for the old place. I was looking for inspiration to write about the first integrated hotel-casino in Las Vegas — again. Slowly driving up to the historic property, I found it pitiful, devastated, although, thank goodness, the rubble of the old buildings had been carted away. I was ashamed for the owners of the 400 West Bonanza Road property. The fire, no doubt, was the stuff of nightmares for the establishment and the new owners. The only things that seemed to remain were the great Moulin Rouge marquee sign at the front of the property, and the old tower. The place didn't look pretty.

The Moulin Rouge now had a fence surrounding the entire perimeter, but I was allowed to drive through the main gate by a black woman attendant. Or was she a security guard? Unannounced, I had showed up and told the attendant that I wanted to speak with the manager. That was good enough for her, I guess. Apparently, she seemed not to have been given any other instructions about what to do with uninvited guests. The attendant also wouldn't tell me her name. After parking, I got out of my vehicle and with my Polaroid camera, I started taking pictures of the marquee sign, much to the chagrin, perhaps, of a property manager, whose name I was to learn later was Len Purdue.

Mr. Purdue rushed out from an adjoining building on the property. He asked me what I was up to. I told him that I was writing a story about the Moulin Rouge. At that point, Mr. Purdue, in his own terse and evasive way, told me to leave, in no uncertain terms, after finally

Side view of the Moulin Rouge with surrounding metal fence, after the devastating arsonist's fire, 2004 (Earnest N. Bracey).

giving me his business card. It seemed Mr. Purdue didn't like reporters or *anyone* writing stories about the Moulin Rouge. Or so I thought. I guessed that any speculation about the new black owners and their intentions was not really appreciated. I left without any further discussion with Mr. Purdue. But I would not be deterred from writing the history of the Moulin Rouge, no matter what.

Those who know about the Moulin Rouge see it as a novelty. The historic site still inspires interest for some, but that interest is not shared by everyone in the Las Vegas community. In fact, most transplanted Las Vegans today have a rudimentary or nebulous understanding of the unfortunate Moulin Rouge. Some see the place as yesterday's news. Admittedly, the hotel-casino's understated charm is no longer evident, and many younger Las Vegans are not familiar with the historical significance of the place, nor do they care whether the Moulin Rouge is rebuilt. But I firmly believe that all Las Vegans should know something about the first interracial hotel-casino in the nation.

No one goes to the Moulin Rouge these days without a specific reason, certainly not for gambling. Before the place burned down, it became "an atmospheric location," or a backdrop for "such period Hollywood productions as the movie 'Casino' and the TV series 'Crime Story.'"[1]

This work is written in the context of the black civil rights movement and black freedom struggle in Las Vegas, Nevada, from the 1950s to 2007. Make no mistake, "the civil rights struggle in Nevada," as professor M.L. Miranda tells us, "was primarily a black struggle," and other minority groups have benefited from this struggle.[2] For many years, black residents stood on the sidelines, especially during the segregation era, while they were summarily shortchanged of their civil rights and civil liberties. Some observers like University of Nevada professor of political science, Michael W. Bowers, say that black Las Vegans are, in many ways, still on the sidelines, as they continue to fight debt and near poverty.

The opportunity to make a living wage or to benefit from the economic prosperity of the city — has not been equally available to all Las Vegas residents. Indeed, in the past, the city was unequivocally wrong about how it treated its black citizens, as white civic officials were not necessarily interested in doing the right thing for the black population, or for impoverished black people. This almost total disregard for the well-being of the black community is an ugly history that must also be told about Las Vegas. Nor should the truth be overshadowed, as blacks have faced unbelievable odds in the city. Of course, when the Moulin Rouge was built, there was something extremely intriguing about the desegregated place, as it once carried a stately air; but it was not an ideal location for such a controversial hotel-casino.

And although the Moulin Rouge was unmatched by any other hotel-casino at that time, and exceeded all expectations, the place was never a Shangri-la. It came to represent both cooperation and conflict between blacks and whites in the Las Vegas community. Indeed, there is no argument among scholars about the racial significance of the Moulin Rouge, as it cultivated strong support in the black community.

Even with its historical and architectural significance, the place today is not a pleasing sight. Still, the Moulin Rouge is too real, too deeply imbedded in the history of Las Vegas to be dismissed outright — or forgotten.

In other words, the historical reality of the place will prevail where its physical structure may not. More fundamentally, whatever success the Moulin Rouge had in the past, it has been a dismal failure in the casino business. Is there some diabolical presence at the place that it has had such bad luck? More importantly, can the Moulin Rouge be exorcised of its unlucky demons? At least as a memory, the place, I believe, will endure, because the name persistently appears in the historical lore of Las Vegas. Therefore, the legacy of the Moulin Rouge remains. Journalist Geoff Schumacher has written that the Moulin Rouge has "earned a treasured place in Las Vegas history, one worthy of preservation,"[3] and hopefully it will rise again.

One can envision a distant revitalization, but it remains to be seen if the Moulin Rouge will rise again, as the new black owners consider what the ill-fated hotel-casino could be. The principals are taking a conservative approach toward the endeavor. But what difference will it make if a new Moulin Rouge is ever built, after all? No doubt, changes at the place will present new opportunities. However, rebuilding the historic property could be a double-edged sword. It could be a way to galvanize or to compromise the black population in Las Vegas. Plus, a new Moulin Rouge would come at a difficult time for the predominantly black community on the west side.

Only time will tell if the fire-ravaged place will be rebuilt. Some see the Moulin Rouge today as just another insignificant resort property, plagued by serious financial woes because of fluctuating market conditions. In any case, perhaps the new black owners would like to build a new, sophisticated hotel-casino with gaming and entertainment in mind.

All in all, the Moulin Rouge mystique remains unique even to this day. The place is still a vital presence in the city, and the final story of the Moulin Rouge has yet to be told. Will the Moulin Rouge hotel and casino fall by the wayside? Is the scandal-ridden place ultimately doomed?

Introduction

Any study of blacks in Las Vegas must start from the premise that black Americans in the state of Nevada have been unjustly treated and discriminated against. This was especially true in an earlier incarnation of the segregated city — that is, in terms of providing equality of opportunity and sharing the tremendous wealth of the burgeoning place. In the early 1950s, for example, the white power structure left black Las Vegans out of any real social or political discussions, largely through discrimination, and the resulting poverty and isolation. Blacks in Las Vegas received limited governmental services during its segregated years. The argument seemed to have been that because some blacks in Las Vegas were neither property owners nor tax-payers, they didn't deserve any public services or consideration. But this did not give city officials the right to discriminate against an entire ethnic group.

This was both distressing and depressing for many black Las Vegans, as they were not given the power to dictate what they wanted their close-knit community to look like. Later, however, black activists fought hard to change things in Las Vegas by marching and demonstrating, and raising their considerable voices. Indeed, as professor of political science Kenneth Minogue tells us, these were black Las Vegans' "only conception of political activity"[1] which could make integration and equality of opportunity come about. This book examines the history of blacks in the city of Las Vegas as it tells the engaging story of the Moulin Rouge, the first integrated hotel and casino in the nation, and those who conceived and built the historic place. There were many who did not like the idea of breaking down the color barrier, or of having an interracial hotel and casino in Las Vegas. Indeed, at that time, it was a revolutionary concept — the notion of providing a sense of racial togetherness and harmony at a hotel-casino.

The Moulin Rouge certainly created controversy. Some thought that building the place was a colossal mistake. As it turned out, "while [the] Moulin Rouge was building and plans [were] being made for an opening that would attract a celebrity-studded crowd of both races, two fiery crosses burned one night out in the nearby valley of Moapa." Apparently, as a stern warning, "both crosses were set up [and ignited] near camps employing" black Americans.[2] It was a cowardly act to say the least; but acceptance of equality wasn't the norm at that time. It is important to note that during this time period, building the Moulin Rouge was an extraordinary achievement, as it increased contact and interaction between blacks and whites in Las Vegas.

This work, however, is also a cautionary tale about what can go wrong with a hotel-casino in Las Vegas, especially one established as a sort of appeasement, making way for racial integration, black equal rights and the city's desegregation efforts. Was it a way to placate the black population? What happened to black people was not right but is a part of the history of Las Vegas. This work, told in the present, is about the racism of the past. It is not a day-to-day account of the Moulin Rouge, but a historical analysis of the place from 1950 to 2007.

Unfortunately, the hotel and casino is not on our national radar or conscience today as it was in the past. For a time, the dream was brought to fruition on a grand scale. Indeed, what was happening in Las Vegas during the 1950s drove the national discussion about racial justice and equality for black Americans. But this emblematic story is complicated, as the city didn't know *any* boundaries when it came to discrimination against blacks. Blacks' disgust and indignation were absolutely justified.

The Moulin Rouge keeps us aware of the specific circumstances of the city's segregated past. Hopefully the Moulin Rouge's story will point the direction that we should take in the future in terms of race-relations. Las Vegas is maybe ashamed of its history of racism and bigotry. But we must be reminded of the city's past in order to transcend it and move forward in the future. As we shall see, the historic Moulin Rouge was buffeted by controversy from its very inception.

The Moulin Rouge started out promisingly enough, particularly because it provided private accommodations to black tourists and entertainers who were being refused such services on the Las Vegas strip, and elsewhere. Indeed, nationally known black entertainers fought along with local black residents for the privilege of staying at many of the posh hotel-casinos on the Las Vegas strip. They too were denied accommodation, even if they were performing and had top billing at the particular property.

White Las Vegans and other visitors wanted to hear and see black artists perform, but white resort and casino bosses did not allow blacks to stay in their segregated hotels and casinos; nor did white business owners extend other services to blacks at restaurants and other public and private establishments. Such discrimination was rampant in Las Vegas, but it also occurred frequently throughout the state of Nevada prior to the 1960s. As the late professor of political science, Elmer Rusco, cogently pointed out, the civil rights movement changed blatantly discriminatory laws, as well as abolished Nevada statutes that prohibited private discrimination, such as segregation in public accommodations, employment, and housing.[3]

Prior to the civil rights movement, the Nevada legislature passed some laws that actually prevented blacks from achieving true equality in Las Vegas. According to some analysts, legislator George Rudiak's 1953 bill to ban racial discrimination in public accommodations was the "initial attack on Las Vegas's de facto segregation." But nothing could be further from the truth. As Rusco accurately wrote:

> The first such bill [banning racial discrimination] was introduced, at the request of the Las Vegas Branch of the National Association for the Advancement of Colored People, in 1939. Similar bills were introduced in 1947 and 1949 also. There was also a 1939 precedent for going to the Las Vegas City Commission to ask for local action against discrimination when the Legislature was unresponsive.[4]

Although we do not have a full account of the civil rights movement in the state of Nevada, the end of discrimination in public accommodations by most casinos in Las Vegas "was brought about by direct negotiations between NAACP leaders" and the gaming or casino industry, not by any "policy stance taken by the city," or by Nevada's 1965 Civil Rights Act.[5] By the mid–60s the Moulin Rouge had gained far more national attention than any other hotel-casino in the state. The place played a vital role in launching the equal rights movement and integration in the city. Indeed, the historic Moulin Rouge, in many respects, empowered the black community, as blacks gained political and economic clout in a city that was a bastion of segregation.

The Moulin Rouge, as the first interracial hotel and casino, provides pedagogical insights into the early relationships between blacks and whites in the city of Las Vegas, demonstrating how blacks struggled for equality and racial parity with white Las Vegans. At that time, blacks in Las Vegas were even denied access to certain neighborhoods, predominantly white areas, for no other reason than their race. Black Las Vegans had problems for years finding decent jobs in the city. And when they did find jobs, especially on the strip, blacks were primarily employed in menial or service jobs, with poverty-scale wages. Unfortunately, blacks also were shut out of top executive positions and casino management; and in many ways, they still are today. Although Don Barden, a wealthy black man, is chairman and chief executive officer of Majestic Investors, operating Fitzgeralds hotel-casino in downtown Las Vegas,[6] he is the exception and not the rule.

But the opening of the Moulin Rouge pioneered jobs and livable wages for black Las Vegans who wanted to work in the casino business. The Moulin Rouge was the heart of the black community on the West side — at least for a little while. And although there were concerns about a rivalry between the respective black and white communities in the city, blacks in Las Vegas were able to beat the odds and early hardships to create a cohesive community that catered to a population that was ignored, or browbeaten and treated unfairly.

The building of the Moulin Rouge was extremely important to the black community. Indeed, its opening was a magical time. Blacks and whites came together in an unlikely location to party, gamble, and to be entertained. But many negative things happened to the black commu-

Front view of the Moulin Rouge marquee sign and signature tower, with steel fence, 2007 (Earnest N. Bracey).

nity in Las Vegas, and the groundbreaking hotel eventually shut down. Many have attributed the first closure of the Moulin Rouge to the opening of "five Strip hotels at the time, changing entertainers and other employee contracts to ban them from after hours jam sessions" that eventually "choked off the life's blood" of the famous place, and "emptied the casino and show-room."[7]

All was not lost because the Moulin Rouge would open again and again. In recent years, though, the Moulin Rouge has struggled. Many would say today that the Moulin Rouge is nothing more than a fleabag hotel off the beaten path of the Las Vegas Strip. Certainly the place could use a serious make-over. The site today is a terrible eyesore in comparison to the elaborate hotels and casinos and upscale properties on the Strip. But the condition of the place today stems from a disastrous fire in 2003, which unfortunately burned most of the Moulin Rouge to the ground. Supporters initially believed that "the long-dormant Moulin

Rouge" would be rescued in 2004 when the Moulin Rouge Development Corporation "bought the property and announced plans for constructing a new Moulin Rouge hotel and casino on the site."[8]

If the hotel and casino is ever rebuilt (for perhaps an estimated $700 million or more), it will also promote the legendary neighborhood surrounding it. Some want to be protected from any new development, but it's been said that the new owners have a different business strategy and they will get things done. Therefore, the black community has been excited at the prospect of an ambitious, new breed of black businessmen buying the Moulin Rouge, moving in, and setting up shop. The black community hopes that the new black owners will "accomplish what could not be done during the casino's heyday [over] five decades ago"—that is, making the place a financial success.[9]

Although the new black entrepreneurs/owners make a convincing case that the dilapidated Moulin Rouge should be resuscitated, they have brought no noticeable improvements to the place, as of this writing. Nothing has been done recently to preserve the original structure. Yet the new black owners have been particularly straightforward, and remain undaunted, taking the long view regarding the Moulin Rouge. They obviously know the full potential of the curious place. Indeed, perhaps the black entrepreneurs "will succeed where so many have failed before because of the experienced team of executives they have gathered and financial backing,"[10] which is so important for the Moulin Rouge to survive. It is optimistic, however, for the new black owners to think that the place can be a success like the Palms and Rio hotels and casinos off the strip in Las Vegas.[11]

The owners believe that the ghosts of the tragic past should be ignored or forgotten. Some believe restoring the Moulin Rouge is an insurmountable task, as it could take a long time for a complete turnaround. Many think that it is prudent to make a fresh start with the irrepressible Moulin Rouge. Some think the new owners should find a new use for the property. In any case, the black businessmen vow to rebuild the place regardless of cost. However, rebuilding the Moulin Rouge at its current location will always be problematic. Yet, revitalization efforts continue on behalf of the new black management. In any event, the place should be preserved because of its trademark architectural and historical significance.

This significance should offer many in the Las Vegas community a tremendous incentive to restore the broken-down Moulin Rouge, no matter the past and current circumstances, as it is a place that is legend in the casino-business history of Las Vegas. But will a new Moulin Rouge really bring new economic resources to the black community? Perhaps one day we will find out. As of this writing, no one knows when construction is expected to begin — if ever. Reconstruction and redevelopment would certainly enable the black owners to do much more for the black community. Will the place ever be restored to its former grandeur? Maybe not, but the Moulin Rouge will always be a part of Las Vegas's legacy.

Even after over fifty years of neglect, the Moulin Rouge has proved an enduring monument to the black equal rights struggle by being recognized as the place where an agreement to end discrimination in the city was made. Was the famous desegregation agreement born of desperation? In addition, the Moulin Rouge still evokes a sense of mystery and awe.

Only time will tell whether the black owners will take advantage of the marvelous opportunity to redevelop the Moulin Rouge, and to make it a mega-resort, like other mega-construction projects going on in Las Vegas. Or does the new ownership mean that the place will eventually be bulldozed over — and we finally lose it forever? Probably not, because the new black owners are also planning a museum and cultural center to preserve the history of the Moulin Rouge.[12] Nonetheless, to pull off the mammoth project to rebuild and restore the place will be a feat in itself, perhaps equal to the original feat of launching the ground-breaking Moulin Rouge.

Chapter One

In the Beginning

It would be difficult to tell *any* story about the Moulin Rouge without discussing its place in the civil rights history of Las Vegas, Nevada. Indeed, it is pretty embarrassing to recall the days when people in Las Vegas were legally segregated and discriminated against because of their ethnic group, skin color, or race. At the same time, this sorry past cannot be forgotten or denied. Yet we can move on and put this unfair and tragic period behind us. That is, if black Las Vegans and others are continuously given the opportunity to share in the wealth, prosperity, and power of the city, and given a chance to build similar or comparable hotel-casinos to those on the famous Strip, and to share in the prosperity of the gaming industry.

It seems almost paradoxical that the Moulin Rouge was built at all. Blacks in Las Vegas, unfortunately, were on the outside looking in. "The Strip casinos were [at one time] totally segregated, [and] off-limits to blacks unless they were the entertainment or labor force."[1] But much has changed in Las Vegas since the opening of the Moulin Rouge, which, as we shall see, was a contentious endeavor, and engendered an unfavorable immediate reaction by known, hardcore racists and bigots in the famous city of lights. Surprisingly, though, Las Vegas "has outgrown the chummy world of the 1950s, when Frank Sinatra and his Rat Pack ruled, [as the city has] turned into a full-blown metropolitan area that is attracting families and businesses from other cities."[2]

Although it seems no one waxes nostalgic about the Moulin Rouge today, it has captured the imagination of those who know something about the first racially integrated hotel-casino in Las Vegas, Nevada, and the nation. Furthermore, the story of the Moulin Rouge began in the early 1950s, when it was determined by the powers-that-be that the time had come for just such an integrated hotel-casino. For years the black community suffered many indignities in silence, as its members were treated like second-class citizens. In fact, they were treated similarly to blacks living in southern states in the 1950s, with Jim Crow laws and racial segregation in full swing.[3]

According to historian Leon F. Litwack, racism, "Negrophobia," and racial segregation in the United States was "deeply rooted in the white psyche" during the 1950s, as "the efforts to separate the races, [and] to quarantine and marginalize" blacks was extended "to every aspect of day-to-day life where blacks and whites came into contact with each other."[4] The discriminatory sentiments or racialist attitudes of Caucasian businessmen and wealthy casino investors, who owned the vast majority of properties on the Las Vegas Strip, further segregated blacks and whites along racial lines. What were the complications that kept blacks and whites apart? Was it all about race?

Unfortunately, among other things, black Americans for the most part could not gamble, be entertained, or stay at the larger, posh hotel and casinos in the great city. Which was ironic, since the public school system in Las Vegas was mostly desegregated.[5] Furthermore, there were noted black leaders in the city, like Dr. James B. McMillan, the first licensed black dentist in Las Vegas and past president of the local National Association for the Advancement of Colored People (NAACP) during the 1960s and 1970s, and Woodrow Wilson, the first black man to serve in the state legislature. These leaders were willing to say forthrightly that it was time to have a modern hotel and casino where blacks could go and spend their money on gambling if they wanted to, as well as be entertained by black stars and headliners of the day. Moreover, in a city where blacks and whites converged in many walks of life and endeavors, it was important to have a place where the two ethnic groups could mix and mingle, without fear of repercussions.

The black population in Las Vegas, of course, thought that an integrated casino-resort, which would eventually be called the Moulin Rouge after the original nightclub in Paris, France,[6] was long overdue. Although the hotel-casino originally attracted comparatively few black patrons, some black customers actually resented the place. Many initially thought that the Moulin Rouge was a faux pas, given that blacks should have been allowed to stay and gamble at *any* Strip hotel. Nevertheless, the Moulin Rouge, inarguably, for many blacks in Las Vegas was instantly gratifying. Some blacks were very enthusiastic about it.

On the other hand, however, many white Las Vegans thought that building an integrated hotel and casino "in a prime location — a site between the predominantly white area of the Strip and the largely black Westside"[7] was pushing the racial-integration envelope of the city at that time too far. Many refused to condone or enthusiastically embrace the idea. Others automatically assumed that blacks in Las Vegas didn't deserve a comparable place for social amusements or public entertainment. There was a feeling of aversion on the part of many white Americans (especially gamblers from the Deep South) who didn't want to be in the presence of a black person, or even to be seated in a parlor of a hotel or at a restaurant with black people.[8] Whites in Las Vegas and in America in general felt they had racial superiority.

It must be clearly understood that many casino industry insiders, white investors, and casino executives, at first doubted that an integrated hotel could be competitive, much less hugely successful. Further, it was thought that white audiences only wanted to admire black performers from afar — not in their own backyard, so to speak. Many felt that it was okay for talented black entertainers to perform for white visitors and tourists at large hotel-casino properties on the Strip, but many judgmental whites refused to associate with blacks, no matter what their social-economic status. Blacks were treated inhumanely and without respect. This Jim Crow racism "not only afflicted ordinary people but black stars as well."[9] Professor William J. Wilson writes that "for whites the most intense forms of racial animosity emerge[d] when blacks compete[d] directly with them for scarce goods or when blacks challenge[d] the very prerogatives (that is, exclusive of prior rights in housing, occupation, education) that have historically set the races apart."[10]

On the other hand, blacks in Las Vegas were defying the legal and traditional sanctions against them and the hold discrimination had on the city. According to Wilson, "the Jim Crow system of segregation was virtually unchallenged until the early 1950s in Las Vegas."[11] Which is to say that the system of segregation in the city of Las Vegas essentially allowed city or local governmental officials to dismiss the concerns of black people, as well as their discontents and injustices. In other words, blacks in the United States were "invisible — hidden in small islands within large cities — unlike European immigrants, and occupied peripheral positions in the region's economy,"[12] especially in Las Vegas.

For a long time, the city fathers of Las Vegas didn't take any interest in the inner lives and struggles of blacks outside the periphery of the Strip. Whether the black menial working force had sufficient resources or led underprivileged lives really didn't matter to the white power structure. Black Las Vegans were ignored in the segregated city. That's how the Las Vegas community dealt with uncomfortable and inconvenient issues of race — at least most of the time. Did the white population have any remorse or pangs of conscience for its superior position, or the shabby treatment of the black population in segregated Las Vegas during the 1950s? Probably not.

Everyone knew that the Strip was an extremely important part of the Las Vegas economy, therefore, black Las Vegans expressed concern that they should have a sophisticated casino-resort for social gatherings besides the many black churches on the Westside. But building such a place for blacks on the Strip was not to be — that is, initially. There is no doubt that it would have been more pragmatic to allow blacks to frequent the hotel-casinos on the Strip, but this was not the case — in the beginning. But, according to journalists Katharine Best and Katharine Hillyer, "some of the strip casino-hotels did [secretly permit] black artists to stay on [their] premises, though it made clear that they [were] not welcome in the actual casinos or restaurants."[13] In other words, some black performers, like Josephine Baker, could stay at a select few of the hotel-casinos, if they were invisible, or hid from the white public, which was a feat in itself. Apparently, Josephine Baker had in her contract that she could stay in any Strip hotel where she was performing.

We need to seriously consider whether black artists with marquee names were treated fairly by such white hotel-casino establishments. The answer is absolutely not, because many black performers had to find overnight and temporary accommodations in black boarding houses or private homes on the predominantly black Westside. Later, following the rise of the Moulin Rouge, "racial barriers on the Strip began to crumble."[14] It would not be an easy or fast transition, even though black Las Vegans totaled over 10 percent of the population in the growing city by 1950.[15] Nevertheless, and "little by little," as professor of history Annelise Orleck has written, "both at the top of the marquee and in the back of the house," so to speak, "segregation [in Las Vegas] began to crack."[16]

Race-relations were changing rapidly, or much more quickly than the local white power structure or white policymakers were willing to accept for fear of losing white clientele and white tourists. Therefore Las Vegas needed a place where blacks could gamble, socialize, interact, and "intermingle with whites without fear" of hateful reverberations.[17] Prior to the opening of the Moulin Rouge, black clubs and bars on the Westside catered exclusively to black servicemen from the Las Vegas Army Air Corps Gunnery School, later the Nellis Air Force Base, and other black patrons. Such places included The New Town and Tavern, Cotton Club, Brown Derby, El Morocco, and Ebony Clubs, which became "hotbeds for late-night entertainment when performers such as Harry Belafonte, Sarah Vaughan, and others appeared at many of these black nights spots after their shows and performances on the [Las Vegas] Strip."[18]

According to Professor Eugene P. Moehring, there was an earlier effort to open an interracial hotel-casino in 1942, when the Horace Heidt Corporation attempted to fashion the Shamrock Hotel downtown as the first place where blacks and whites could commingle — eat, dance, and drink together. It failed miserably because belligerent whites vehemently protested,[19] opposing such an unprecedented and disagreeable move. Therefore, the city officials denied the Shamrock Hotel an operating permit because of Jim Crow policies, and perhaps because of their racist fears of an integrated crowd, which was, no doubt, considered very taboo.[20]

Over a decade later, the winds of change in Las Vegas took hold in the slow-to-progress city, when in 1954, Will Max Schwartz and other

Former heavyweight boxing champion Joe Louis, one of the former owners of the Moulin Rouge, pulls a slot, 1955 (Nevada State Museum and Historical Society, Las Vegas).

white private investors considered an inclusive, interracial hotel. Perhaps these men had the foresight to know what would happen. The only thing that seemed certain at that time was that the hotel would finally be built. It has been reported that the Moulin Rouge was built for "an estimated $6.9 million,"[21] but it was actually constructed for approximately $3.5 million,[22] which was still a considerable amount of money for the time — a small fortune, in fact. Schwartz held a 38 percent interest in the place, while the other principal partners were Alexander Bisno, a Los Angeles investment broker who owned a 31 percent share of the venture, and Louis Ruben, a New York restaurant owner, who held 29 percent of the Moulin Rouge.[23]

The remaining 2 percent ownership of the business was supposedly held by the former heavyweight boxing champion Joe Louis, who apparently held some stock in the hotel as well, but this has never been officially verified. Eventually, Joe Louis became an official host and greeter at the place, and continued for many years before he died in 1981. According to award-winning film director and author Trish Geran, Joe Louis "was placed in that position so the hotel [Moulin Rouge] could attract wealthy blacks,"[24] which it eventually did do. But when the glitzy Moulin Rouge opened its doors on May 24, 1955, it became "an extremely popular night spot, a $3.5 million showplace for black and white entertainers, as well as the Mecca and must-see tourist attraction for black Americans who wanted to have fun, dine, gamble, and visit in Las Vegas. It also reflected the evolving role of race in American society, as well as the tentative first steps for southern Nevada on its long and tortuous road to anything remotely resembling equal opportunity."[25]

Chapter Two

The Inevitability of Interracial Socialization in Las Vegas

The initial planning and erecting of the Moulin Rouge hotel and casino proved to be an enormous challenge in Las Vegas, as blacks in the city sought equality and social justice, and white businessmen and developers finally decided to construct the place, regardless of the circumstances. In fact, building the Moulin Rouge has been described as "among the most daunting development projects" in the history of Las Vegas.[1] Indeed, devising the Moulin Rouge hotel and casino was easier said than done, especially when you had to consider the tension and racial climate in 1954. But when the city's planning commission eventually gave the white business developers the green light to build, the suggested project seemed more viable.

Equally significant for the white financiers of the proposed Moulin Rouge, the hotel and casino would become a way to generate income. What was probably the first purchase of real estate in Las Vegas specifically to provide recreational facilities for things like gambling and entertainment for both blacks and whites would prove to be monumental. As one local reporter writes, the Moulin Rouge would create "a precedent for interracial socialization" in Las Vegas.[2] Therefore, the place became the landmark development project in the black Westside neighborhood, on what at the time seemed an insignificant piece of land.

In 1954 no one thought that the Moulin Rouge would become "the center of black culture of Las Vegas."[3] Indeed, the Westside would eventually explode on the scene in Las Vegas with black cultural traditions from across the United States. It became notable for the black community's antagonistic disregard of the city's racism and continuing discrimination. As Dr. Bob Bailey, a black activist who would become "a major factor in fighting discrimination," in Las Vegas tells us:

> What happened of course was the arrival of many of us from different parts of the country, that were able to bring about change through various different methods. [Indeed], the effort had been put forth here to garner civil rights legislation, and that was the prevalent force across the country at that time. A constituency had formed here that we actually came and looked into, to support the efforts that were ongoing.[4]

Needless to say, planning and constructing the Moulin Rouge was not some sinister move by unscrupulous people, as blacks in Las Vegas themselves continued to push for drastic changes and a viable place like the Moulin Rouge. As already discussed, the Moulin Rouge was not the first effort by white businessmen to develop an integrated establishment in the city. As the late Woodrow Wilson said:

> In the real early days here we had total discrimination in all the establishments in uptown Las Vegas and the small Strip area. We had only one or two hotels on the Strip at that time. So we were defeated when the city commission voted to deny Horace Heidt a license [for an interracial hotel].... It would have helped to raise the economic status of the community because that would have put blacks in positions of authority, management and the like by having people make the type of money that executives and sub-executives make in the hotel industry.[5]

In so many words, the city of Las Vegas continued its racial restrictions against blacks in 1954 because of racism. As one white Las Vegan was quoted as saying, "Sure we Jim Crow [blacks] ... [because] we think that's the way it should be by nature." The self-satisfied white man goes on, perhaps matter-of-factly, to state that "mixing of races could never work here. We just don't want it, that's all. So we keep the Negro in [his] place."[6] Nonetheless, blacks persevered, and without hesitation, pressured the city of Las Vegas for their constitutional rights, insisting that everyone be treated equally, and with respect. Contrary to the high expectations of blacks newly arrived to the city, their insistence did not initially make a significant difference in Las Vegas. Yet, blacks fought on, demanding their constitutional rights. According to political historian Robert A. Goldwin:

> The unspoken principles — at least unspoken in the Constitution — are that rights are inherent in individuals, not in the groups they belong to; that we are all equal as human beings in the sense that no matter what our color, sex, national origin, or religion, we are equal in the possession of the rights that governments are instituted to protect; and that as a consequence, the only source of legitimate political power is the consent of the governed.[7]

Unfortunately, the city government of Las Vegas failed in its constitutional mandate to protect the black population. White governmental officials infringed upon the constitutional rights of blacks on a daily basis, and without, apparently, any remorse. In this troubled and adversarial atmosphere, "the foundation of the Moulin Rouge was being set," and finally constructed, "as Brown v. Board of Education opened the doors to the [eventual] dismantling of segregation" in Las Vegas.[8] However, before integration would take hold or become commonplace, West Las Vegas became the nerve center for the black population in the city, as the area would provide all the essentials of life. This was surprising considering blacks had at one time settled in an area called Carver Park in Henderson, Nevada, near the now-defunct Basic Magnesium Plant. It was a major source of employment for blacks during World War II.

Carver Park "was later abandoned by [black] Americans because the place did not provide for a social life for blacks." Many blacks deliberately moved "to the Westside or the old McWilliams Townsite west of the [main] railroad tracks in Las Vegas."[9] To be sure, "it was a time when the Westside grew from a settlement into a community, when Nevada's first black professionals migrated to the area and became prominent community leaders."[10]

Black professionals were also slowly becoming the role models in the black community of Las Vegas, as many built their homes in the more affluent sections of the Westside area, like Berkeley Square, which is located between D and H, and Fremont and Burns.[11] The late black historian and University of Nevada professor Roosevelt Fitzgerald put it this way:

> By the time the 1950s got underway, the Westside had not only developed into a sizeable black residential community but it had also developed a thriving district. The latter experienced its success due directly to the presence of segregation in Las Vegas proper. Most of the businesses [however] were marginal; barber shops, beauty shops, night clubs, soda shops, small cafes, pool rooms and corner grocery stores. A few professionals such as medical doctors and dentists were also present. Several of the homes built there, without the assistance of mortgage companies and banks, were constructed with the black entertainer in mind.[12]

Fitzgerald's assessment of this time and place is correct; and for many years black entertainers were the life blood of the Westside, as they brought in substantial revenue to the businesses of the black community. West Las Vegas, indeed, would become a place that everyone who visited the city wanted to see. The place where the other half—the blacks—lived. They wanted to experience, perhaps, the racial ambience and dichotomy of the city. Of course, the black community was where the action was in terms of black entertainment. The neighborhood always looked alive at that time, like it was a living, breathing entity as people bustled about—day and night. For some, visiting the black neighborhood in Las Vegas became a sort of ritual. Some white tourists even in the 1950s began to discover the magical place called the Westside.

But the white casino bosses, as well as "eastern and Midwestern mobsters" who owned several businesses in Las Vegas, squirmed at the very idea of white customers traveling over to the black neighborhood to hear black musicians and entertainers perform, especially at the minimally sophisticated but numerous black clubs and bars. Apparently, many visiting whites were willing to take the risk, if there really was any, to soak in the nightlife of the Westside. The local white population reacted with increasing hostility toward blacks, and against those who associated with black people, because racism and discrimination reflected the true reality in the city. White casino bosses and white businessmen wanted all who ventured outside the confines of white society to know that that was beyond the bounds of respectability.

Nonetheless, the economy was booming on the Westside, fueled largely by tourists, locals and black entertainers, who insisted upon being treated fairly and like human beings, especially when they were visible to the public. This was despite the fact that the white power structure went on to do everything it could to harass the black residents of Las Vegas and their occasional white visitors. Still, the black neighborhood continued to explode with its black musical and entertainment traditions, as the Westside rapidly moved forward, despite racial segregation. But the most interesting thing about the black area of West Las Vegas was what the public couldn't see — or understand.

Although black Las Vegas differed from the predominantly white, master-planned communities, in many important respects, black areas resembled them in significant ways. Both communities and their respective residents worked for similar businesses (i.e., the separate nightclubs, restaurants, and casino industries). Nevertheless, blacks in Las Vegas lived in an entirely different world, with special patterns of behavior, special attitudes — especially in terms of politics — and different ways of thinking. Unfortunately, "whites were more likely to invoke prejudices as societies grew more complex and competitive, thereby denying [blacks] full access to opportunities and resources."[13] Still, Jim Crow racism governed all facets of black people's lives in Las Vegas.

Fortunately, though, racism and prejudice were not so strong that they couldn't be overcome, and many thought things had to change. The vast majority of black people in Las Vegas, during the 1950s, were not wealthy as a group — even given the prosperity of the city. More importantly, the racially diverse demographics and "shifting patterns" were "fueled not by broad social changes but almost exclusively by the valley's" predicted growth, which would eventually "cut across racial and economic lines."[14]

Therefore, more than just an idea, the Moulin Rouge in West Las Vegas became a strategically important location where black entertainers, banned from the Strip hotel-casinos, would one day be treated like the stars they truly were. Some in the city of Las Vegas would even come

The Moulin Rouge before the grand opening, 1955 (Nevada State Museum and Historical Society, Las Vegas).

to see the building of the Moulin Rouge as an absolute necessity, particularly for favorable race relations.[15] Clearly, "even well-meaning [white] Nevada politicians [and white citizens] historically have misunderstood the [emerging] black population" of Las Vegas,[16] especially in their attitudes about the historic Moulin Rouge venture. Consequently, as things would begin to change for the black community, such as the building of the Moulin Rouge hotel and casino (in a nondescript place at that time), an ongoing tug-of-war began with the city and white power structure in Las Vegas, as we shall see later in this work.

But progress toward a local system incorporating equality for blacks in the white casino industry in Las Vegas wasn't in the cards in 1954. In the final analysis, one must understand that as blacks in the city and in the casino industry in particular tried to improve their status, this led to a period of racial tensions. The new Moulin Rouge hotel and casino stood in the immediate, awkward foreground. It took some serious finagling on the part of the white developers to even get the first brick laid, and much more for whites in Las Vegas to psychologically accept the place.

Chapter Three

The Main Event

Many in Las Vegas at the time of its building felt that the Moulin Rouge hotel and casino would never be a really classy operation — that is, in comparison to other opulent hotel properties on the Strip. But for its time, the hotel, modeled after the defunct Sands, was contemporary, and as palatial as any Strip casino-hotel. Indeed, the once swanky Moulin Rouge, according to the late Nevada historian Gary Elliott, was "strikingly beautiful and comparable in elegance to any Strip competitors."[1] More importantly, the classy Moulin Rouge, "offered all the gaming, entertainment, and comfort that could be found anywhere" in the state of Nevada, and it was "as plush as *any* hotel on the Strip and proved that a mixed-race crowd could enjoy themselves."[2] The quirky place certainly had charm and character in the beginning.

The biggest lesson in opening the Moulin Rouge was to learn how blacks and whites could get along in a social setting. The night the doors of the place opened was a special experience, a momentous occasion, an extravaganza, a marquee event during a turbulent era of race relations in American history. But it is and was incorrect to think that the Moulin Rouge was only created to serve some revolutionary social purpose. Elliott tells us that the hotel was in no uncertain terms, "constructed, opened, and operated to make a profit."[3]

The Moulin Rouge, nonetheless, became particularly symbolic for blacks before and after it opened, especially in light of Las Vegas's racist past. Journalist Kristi Goodwin writes that "because of the equal access it provided blacks, the Moulin Rouge became a symbol of the times, a monument to their expanding civil rights."[4] The Moulin Rouge, despite what has been written to the contrary, was indeed established to make a point, becoming an emblem of change, integration, and equality among Las Vegas's hotels and casinos. But clearly the first white owners, as mentioned, "had no particularly altruistic intentions [such as improving race relations] when they opened the hotel and nightclub; they were in it for the money."[5]

The result of the opening of the legendary Moulin Rouge was a vibrant nightlife for blacks living in the resort city, as "it catered to a totally interracial group of people from Las Vegas, from Hollywood, and from throughout the U.S."[6] Until the opening, "black tourism [per se] was non-existent,"[7] but this situation would quickly change. The standing room, jaw-droppingly unbelievable opening night, as already mentioned "was a gala affair hosted by Joe Louis and [featured great] performances by the Platters and flashy chorus-line routines,"[8] which emphasized the "good-times" atmosphere of the place. Within the next several months the Moulin Rouge began to stage some shows that "were among the best in the city,"[9] and the world. The hotel was indeed the place to be. Goodwin writes that "elegantly wardrobed chorus girls performed the cancan; black headliners such as Harry Belafonte and Sammy Davis, Jr., [barred from Strip hotels and casinos] appeared at late night jam sessions. [And] newer stars like Gregory Hines made their debut" at the fledgling Moulin Rouge.[10]

The amazing place was almost perfect, like a racially integrated Camelot, a dream world, which empowered and employed many blacks — as well as whites — as hosts, showroom banquet waiters, exotic Watusi dancers, and kitchen help. The glamorous, all-black stage show during the opening of the Moulin Rouge "included eight dancers, six showgirls, and four male dancers."[11] The white owners of the Moulin Rouge also hired some of the best waiters from among first-class hotels across the nation, who "served international gourmet cuisine," sumptuous and gastronomic meals in "the Deauville Room, while wearing immaculate tuxedos with [spotless] white gloves."[12] It was probably an amazing sight. A classy operation was the name of the game for the fledgling hotel-casino and its owners, and they spared no expense.

Although the eye-catching Moulin Rouge consisted of only two

The famous cancan dancers at the Moulin Rouge during one of their routines, 1955 (Nevada State Museum and Historical Society, Las Vegas).

main stuccoed buildings at the time of its celebrated opening, it had 110 rooms and a gorgeous showroom, swimming pool, restaurant/coffee shop, dress-shop, and bar, which was constructed of highly polished and expensive hardwoods. There was also a terrific lounge, theater, and a casino. And before it was even in vogue, the Moulin Rouge stocked some of the finest clothing fashions available to patrons at that time, according to the reflections of Hazel Gay, one of the dress shop operators during the 1950s.[13]

Almost overnight, the popularity of the Moulin Rouge grew exponentially. It was an auspicious sign. The crazy place became insanely popular, making the Moulin Rouge synonymous with intrigue and fun, as "politicians, celebrities, and high-rollers peppered the audience."[14]

The famous mural behind the bar at the Moulin Rouge during its heyday (Nevada State Museum and Historical Society, Las Vegas).

Orleck writes that "the Moulin Rouge quickly acquired a reputation as the place in Las Vegas where big-name black and white entertainers could hobnob, play music and perform on the same stage. Westside regulars Frank Sinatra and Dean Martin were followed there by Tallulah Bankhead, Bob Hope, Milton Berle, and jazz bandleaders Tommy and Jimmy Dorsey."[15]

It was extremely important to the white owners that people felt comfortable coming to the showy place. By any measure, race-relations were not ambiguous at the establishment. For instance, black and white entertainers, who would occasionally drop by at the Moulin Rouge, often gave impromptu performances, if the mood struck them, after the main stage events. It was all, indeed, a trailblazing endeavor. *Life Magazine* glorified the Moulin Rouge by emblazoning lovely black American showgirls dressed in full costume from its opening on the June 20, 1955, cover, with their sparkling, elaborate headdresses, very short frilled dresses, and lace garters to hold up their silk, fishnet stockings. Shapely legs with petticoats gave their trademark cancan kicks in a freeze-frame pose for black historical posterity.

The white owners had created a one-of-a-kind place that maximized black talent and aped the most luxurious hotels and casinos of the day; and it proved to be an antidote to what ailed segregated Las Vegas, at least for a time. Blacks and whites from all over didn't miss the opportunity to experience the wonderful, racial ambience. The Moulin Rouge "jumped around the clock ... particularly late at night following the last shows at other clubs downtown and on the Strip," according to Tom Flagg.[16] Flagg goes on to quote the late University of Nevada professor Roosevelt Fitzgerald: "Black entertainers and white entertainers, who had known each other for years and worked on the same stages found that only at the Moulin Rouge could they socialize together. People never knew what big names they were going to see at the Rouge. Musicians would go up on the stage and sit in with who ever was playing."[17]

Therefore, the Moulin Rouge was a place for almost *everyone*, but it would become even more controversial because of its increasing popularity. Indeed, the hot night spot, "because of the quality of the outstanding entertainment, such as performances by the Rat Pack in its heyday," became so popular — a legendary "third show" was added to accommodate the growing and demanding crowds.[18] The Moulin Rouge also became the entertainment place to go if you wanted to see (sometimes by chance) such famous stars as Louis Armstrong, Joey Bishop, Nat King Cole, Jack Benny, Peter Lawford, and Sammy Davis, Jr. — that is, "after their gigs and closing hours on the Strip" at 2 A.M.[19]

At first, many of the powers-that-be saw the place as inconsequential. But later the Moulin Rouge, as we shall see, was put at odds with the major Strip casinos because of its increasing popularity and success. The goings-on at the popular place did not go unnoticed. The Moulin Rouge "boasted a large black and white clientele, defying racist policies in other establishments which precluded blacks from frequenting any business where they could sit down."[20] Thus, the popular place was taking in money from almost every ethnic group, and taking business away from every casino in town.

Indeed, the continuing operation of the Moulin Rouge ran counter to the white casinos' interest in making the Las Vegas Strip the main focus of the city — social and political implications notwithstanding — because "the lavish, relaxed, integrated atmosphere along with the stellar clientele drew increasingly larger crowds from the downtown and [affluent] Strip properties."[21] And white casino owners were definitely beginning to feel the heat of competition. But there were obviously other political pressure. So when the Moulin Rouge was completed, and effectively up and running, it started to derail focus on the future Las Vegas Strip.

The local white power structure felt that Las Vegas could just as easily do without the place. Wary and perhaps jealous, some white casino owners even "ordered their employees not to patronize" the Moulin Rouge."[22] But such a command did not sit well, or stop white workers and showgirls from the Strip casinos from frequenting the Moulin Rouge.

The city officials showed no foresight and no fortitude in not letting the black population fully integrate the major properties on the Strip.

The first integrated hotel-casino in Las Vegas, therefore, provided the city with a rare opportunity to critically examine itself— and make things right for its black citizens and tourists while segregation was still being legally enforced, and where daily inequities existed in a racially split community. In fact, several state assembly bills designed to bar discrimination in public places failed in the 1950s,[23] primarily because black activists were unable to effectively lobby for their constitutional and fundamental rights. Blacks were not taken seriously, and largely ignored. But the Moulin Rouge provided "the spark needed to bring an end to segregation on the Strip."[24] According to Geran, blacks in Las Vegas, nonetheless, felt that the place "was their first major accomplishment in Las Vegas and the Westside's showplace."[25]

The Moulin Rouge, in other words, illuminated the race-relations problems in the glittering city of lights in the 1950s. And the fact that blacks in Las Vegas were being denied their fundamental rights, freedom, civil liberties, and equal protection under the laws, was spotlighted for all the world to see. It was amazing to think that a place for gaming and entertainment could be constructed which would cater to this search for rights after years of struggle by black residents for dignity, identity — and their desire for a better way of life — while recognizing the city's inglorious past in terms of race-relations.

Chapter Four

After the Lights and Fanfare

The Moulin Rouge is an extremely important Las Vegas casino site because it gives us a real notion about what really happened in the city, especially in terms of race relations. It also gives structure to our understanding of the city's Jim Crow past. The heightened status of the place came as a complete surprise, but the first integrated hotel-casino, as already mentioned, was so successful "that the casinos on the Strip were abandoned after midnight because almost everyone — including employees — headed to West Las Vegas,"[1] to the Moulin Rouge. It was actually considered an insult by the white casino bosses when even well-known white stars decided to spend time at the Moulin Rouge, testing the racist system.

The outrageous response of the Las Vegas casino bosses cannot be exaggerated. White-owned "restaurants and casinos often displayed signs [like] "No-colored trade solicited,"[2] which was typical of what was occurring throughout most of the southern states in the 1950s. Racial discrimination and segregation in public and private accommodations are not what this country is about, but these things did exist in Las Vegas. In fact, the city, as well as the state, "generally responded to national events rather than becoming a leader in abolishing discrimination in accommodations, employment, and housing."[3] Indeed, the black population was shown exactly how insignificant it was by the adverse, exclusive district policies established by the city and Las Vegas resorts.

Even more importantly, because of the Jim Crow laws, the first plans for the historic Moulin Rouge were downright rejected by the city officials. Some white Las Vegans appeared to be unhappy with the decision to move forward, despite complaints from blacks. As with any other business that catered to both blacks and whites, the arguments against the place reflected the hostilities of prejudiced people for the black population in the city. And even though the Moulin Rouge was built in the Westside, the location was still not enough to assuage the concerns of whites who lived close by.

After Moulin Rouge opened, there was also the concern that its very success would diminish the properties on the Las Vegas Strip. Some scholars doubt this, because the Westside was certainly a most unexpected locale to find a hotel-casino, given the isolated setting. But blacks were "shunned by the Jim Crow policies of the half-dozen resorts then open on the Strip."[4] So what did it really mean to establish such an enigmatic place? The actual construction of the Moulin Rouge, of course, was a point of no return; but some saw the place as a recipe for disaster. Indeed, it seemed that the only clear beneficiaries of the racially integrated Moulin Rouge, when it first opened its big doors, were the owners, or those who had a stake in the place.[5]

The 1955 opening was during the zenith of new hotel-casinos in Las Vegas. Indeed, the Moulin Rouge and other new hotel-casinos, especially on the Strip in Las Vegas, took the same sort of approach — build small — until the advent of the mega-resort, which radically changed the way people gambled. The aim was to make risk or gambling more addictive and entertaining. Later, the elimination of segregation in all hotel-casinos, for a more inclusive gaming atmosphere, would slowly take shape.

As we have seen, the black community in Las Vegas eventually rallied around the Moulin Rouge project, because it brought social awareness to the condition of blacks in the city, as they struggled against racial subordination. But the creation of the Moulin Rouge was not a collaborative effort between the black community and its white owners. How did the owners overcome the initial challenges in starting the hotel-casino, particularly when the Moulin Rouge was built on the pretext of only making money? The white owners accepted the inevitability that people would come to the place.

As mentioned, the place evoked feelings of a good time, as it welcomed people from all places, backgrounds, cultures, and ethnic groups. The Moulin Rouge, moreover, revealed much about what was taking place in Las Vegas. But no one could have imagined that the historic hotel-casino would become a symbol of the black neighborhood. Blacks in Las Vegas felt a deep sense of connection to the unlikely attraction—a sort of solidarity or interconnectiveness. Eventually, the Moulin Rouge would become the center of gambling life for blacks before desegregation. In fact, some black locals and tourists were actually excited by the notable success of the place; however, some blacks were not so enthusiastic.

The Moulin Rouge would come to have a more practical purpose than gambling or attracting tourism: it was a place where many com-

Stump and Stumpy relaxing at the Moulin Rouge with Rosita Davis, 1955 (Nevada State Museum and Historical Society, Las Vegas).

munity events and meetings would be held to grapple with the different issues confronting the black population in the city of Las Vegas — something that had never been done before, as blacks began to ratchet up their expressions of concern, protest, and displeasure. Black citizens had to become more self-reliant to survive, since the city of Las Vegas seemed not to care about helping the black community. It wasn't because blacks didn't want to become a part of the larger community, as the whole city struggled with Jim Crow racism. But as we will later see, gradually, times were changing in Las Vegas.

The Moulin Rouge was known mostly for its fantastic entertainment. According to journalist Richard Todd, "the new wisdom in Las Vegas is that people don't come ... for the gambling, they come for 'entertainment.'"[6] Indeed, before the 1960s, the American public's conception of hotel-casinos was intimate spaces and easy, fun-loving times, while tourists shared musicals, dancing entertainment and exquisite meals, in mostly cosmopolitan dining areas. And the Moulin Rouge was no exception. As the late University of Nevada professor, Roosevelt Fitzgerald once wrote:

> White and black entertainers who performed in the larger hotels began to congregate at the Moulin Rouge after they would have completed their final performance for the evening. White patrons of those hotels followed them to the Rouge and that had a negative impact on the income of those other establishments. Ultimately it caused them to establish policies which required the entertainers and the show-girls to remain on the premises for a certain length of time following the second show.[7]

The rave reviews for the showroom entertainment at the Moulin Rouge were second to none. The historic hotel casino became unwanted competition for the Strip casinos, as that entire area "was almost dark after 11 o'clock." Almost tranquil. In a revelatory 2000 interview, Sarann Knight-Preddy, one of the first black owners, recalled, "Someone on the Strip got the bug and said the Moulin Rouge needed to close down.... I don't know how much stock to put in that, but everybody working there [on the Strip] believed it."[8] The Moulin Rouge would close down, but for less obvious and pernicious reasons. Nevertheless, some blacks throughout the nation could not wait to attend the nighttime shows or visit the place to see the various Hollywood movie stars and entertainment.

Part of the appeal of the Moulin Rouge, of course, was that the specialized hotel-casino was unusual, an extraordinary attraction. Indeed, the legendary place took on mythic dimensions. After visiting during the late 1950s, many felt that they had taken part in something very special and different. Many stated that it was thoroughly enjoyable, memorable—like a spiritual experience. The iconic Moulin Rouge certainly drew large crowds in the manner of a religious revival. Some of the interest was simply personal and because of the novelty. But the mystery and actual power of the place resonated with black people, and many whites. Some might even say that the Moulin Rouge is a sacred place.

The Moulin Rouge was awe-inspiring, timeless in the sense that it very much evoked feelings of grandeur or spirituality. In the not-too-distant future, for instance, the New Hope Christian Church would "operate out of the Moulin Rouge's storeroom, drawing some 300 congregants each Sunday,"[9] until it finally closed. Furthermore, visiting the Moulin Rouge for many blacks became sort of like a pilgrimage, especially for black tourists, entertainers, and high-stakes gamblers. Indeed, it became like a once-in-a-lifetime obligation for some blacks in the United States who were looking for a resort experience they never had in their lives.

For some the Moulin Rouge was a revered place of introspection located on a sacred site. And for others, visiting the Moulin Rouge harked back to a time and place when tourists were not that concerned about losing their money—or taking a chance at the casinos tables. According to journalist Jay Tolson, "Places are sacred according to how the sacred is understood." Tolson goes on to state that "human societies have understood the sacred in ways that are both distinctive to their age and enduring constant."[10] In this respect, the Moulin Rouge endured. In a way, it is a mystical legend, a place to behold. Indeed, it was a crossroad or stopover for some who traveled by automobile to California. A stop at the Moulin Rouge was the thing to do while in Las Vegas.

The effect of the Moulin Rouge can be compared to Jackie Robinson's integration of the American professional baseball league, an overwhelming event. So yes, some might have considered the Moulin Rouge a sacred place. The desegregated hotel-casino meant that black people didn't have to look over their shoulders anymore when gambling, and they had a place for community and special events. In this regard, the Moulin Rouge revolutionized the face of Las Vegas in terms of race relations.

Although Las Vegas became the place for a uniquely American conception — the mega-hotel-casino, or mega-resort — the power of the Moulin Rouge was rooted in its aesthetics, or its "fantasy architecture."[11] The ambience was decidedly different from some hotel-casinos. Unlike other popular hotel-casinos during their heyday, the Moulin Rouge created an unprecedented interest and excitement because of its unusual buildings. These allowed the owners and managers to let employees work realistically, openly, and cooperatively, as well as play in a conducive, friendly environment. As Todd tells us, "Whatever the architecture does for the gambling [in the city of Las Vegas], there is little doubt that the gambling enhances the architecture — it provides the charge in the air, the sense of living dangerously, that keeps the place from being the Disney World it sometimes seems to want to become."[12]

But perhaps this was not the case in the 1950s, as casinos like the Moulin Rouge struggled to make it, to find their identities. Clearly, building the Moulin Rouge showed the shifting social and political and racial landscapes in Las Vegas. Increasing their political clout was a major concern for blacks in the city. Discrimination, of course, loomed large. To some extent, there was an opportunity for casinos in Las Vegas to take the leadership role in providing jobs to blacks, but many white-owned casinos on the Strip and downtown hindered the causes of fairness, social justice, and economic opportunity. The reality was that some blacks allowed themselves to be duped by some of the white-owned hotel-casinos into taking low-paying jobs, because of desperation. These actions should have been embarrassing to the white city fathers, especially because the local government allowed casinos and other businesses to get away with discrimination, but many didn't feel any remorse.

Some of the major Strip casinos were fundamentally irresponsible when it came to the black population, which was unproductive and counterintuitive. Other hotel-casinos in Las Vegas had a dismal black hiring record. The scarcity of black Americans in high ranking casino positions wasn't even addressed. In the long run, blacks in Las Vegas would have to make personal financial sacrifices almost every day. One of the many potential consequences of not hiring blacks for Strip casino jobs—and the abrupt firing of many—was outright protest by black Las Vegans. The firing of some blacks was a devastating loss for their families. Still, some blacks working for white-owned hotel-casinos would take comfort in the fact that they would eventually get support from the federal government.

Some blacks in Las Vegas felt that white residents owed them something for the past discrimination. Some whites in Las Vegas at that time, however, questioned the legality of the federal government infringing on their ability to hire who they wanted, especially when it concerned states' rights and the gambling industry.[13] "The loosely knit nature of the city permitted a great deal of privacy, mobility, and personal choice" for white people and their casino businesses.[14] Meanwhile, blacks in Las Vegas were dehumanized, which opened up the floodgates of racial inequality and blatant racism.

As we shall see, little attention was being paid to the concerns of blacks in the city. And the mistreatment of blacks, it seemed, was hardly noticed. According to journalist James Goodrich, "the whites of Las Vegas overwhelmingly support[ed] racial prejudice and [made] no bones about it."[15] Apparently, white citizens did not recognize that they were hurting black people, as many did absolutely nothing in terms of supporting the black community, especially if they were teetering on economic ruin. And as we shall see, "the deep-seated prejudice did not seem to decrease [initially] among whites, and the pace of integration was agonizingly slow."[16]

Therefore, much can be learned from what was happening at the Moulin Rouge in terms of fairness in providing jobs and racial equality, or equality of opportunity. In fact, the grandiosity of the place had become a focal point, as the hotel-casino cashed in on people's appetite for entertainment and gambling. Little did anyone know that the Moulin Rouge's contribution would become legendary. No one can question the influence of the Moulin Rouge on the city of Las Vegas. And for a short time, the place captured the imagination of our nation. In the coming years, as will be discussed in the rest of this book, people would cringe at the discombobulation of the Moulin Rouge, especially as the white power structure would begin to slowly dismantle "the barriers erected to limit participation in their economic boom."[17] Many during this period scratched their heads in frustration and amazement. But what mattered most was that the Moulin Rouge was a great undertaking in the city of Las Vegas, because of the message it would convey — a commitment to racial equality.

The Moulin Rouge exceeded expectations, but it was not developing "any long range economic viability."[18] And sooner rather than later, the euphoria over the place began to wane. The historic hotel-casino, however, set the tone for the ensuing years in terms of a heated racial and political climate, which was not always positive. Richard B. Taylor, a local author and white businessman, would eventually be able to lease and operate the Moulin Rouge,[19] until it was abruptly sold. The first racially integrated hotel-casino would survive for a short period "mainly on weekly and monthly occupants ... probably newcomers to Las Vegas seeking jobs in the downtown area of the city."[20] Finally, as we will learn later, selling the Moulin Rouge would leave a small margin for disingenuousness, since there would be little time for reflections on racial and cultural ambiguities.

Chapter Five

The New Business Acquisition

Despite the early success of the Moulin Rouge, few believed that the place would be successful over the long haul. And many were right on that point. The Moulin Rouge eventually failed for a variety of reasons after the initial fanfare. But the opening of the Moulin Rouge must be seen for its historical context, even though the place was short-lived. As one can imagine, the building of the first interracial resort in Las Vegas, which "was nearly as segregated as any [place] in the South,"[1] led to a sense of urgency, mainly because of the restlessness and disappointment of blacks living in the city of lights — in their depressed neighborhoods (mainly on the Westside), and in ramshackle or dilapidated homes.

Something had to give. During the 1960s, an increasing number of blacks began to question the value of interracial cooperation and noted the efficacy of violent protests, rather than placing "greater emphasis on racial cohesiveness as the mechanism to promote black advancement."[2] Although the interracial cooperation at the Moulin Rouge was not exactly the panacea for all that ailed the black population in Las Vegas, it had a dramatic and profound effect on the racial politics and climate of the city. The glamorous Moulin Rouge became a place where blacks could go and feel at home in the racist city. They could brag about the place, as if it were their own, as a subjugated, repressed and despised people. As professor Shelby Steel has astutely written, "One of the few advantages of belonging to a despised group is that you so clearly owe nothing to your oppressor."[3] This type of thinking was perhaps the predominant and most unfortunate attitude of many black people living in Las Vegas prior to 1960. Sociology professor William J. Wilson also succinctly writes that

> racial hostility among blacks stems from beliefs that they have been forced into marginal, ambiguous, or insecure positions. It really doesn't matter that the degree of bitterness does not always correspond with the extent of racial suppression. What is important, in the final analysis, is the way blacks perceive both their inferior status and the efforts of whites to keep them in subordinate positions.4

The most important thing to keep in mind, however, is that the fabulous and popular Moulin Rouge hotel and casino "contributed to the civil rights movement generally, and prepared the way for integration that came to Las Vegas in 1960."[5] But was the city culpable in not doing enough for its black citizens — that is, was the local government doing everything that it was supposed to do for all its residents? Absolutely not. Perhaps blacks in the community were not considered legitimate Las Vegans. And there seemed to be no way that the divergent black and white communities could be unified.

Nevertheless, as Wilson tells us, "The first seven years of the turbulent 1960s marked a period of black optimism and active protest against racial injustice,"[6] which will be briefly discussed later in this chapter.

Indeed, blacks were beginning to protest loudly in Las Vegas, as it was the only way many felt they could be heard, or could continue their budding efforts to integrate the city. In other words, the black population took radical, direct action to change things along racial lines. Tellingly, many black people and white activists were involved in the civil rights movement in Southern Nevada, which was considered the "Mississippi of the West," because of its blatant, race-based discrimination in public accommodations and employment, as well as its despicable racism, which existed in almost all social and political matters concerning blacks.

Indeed, there was a hard layer of racial prejudice just below the sandy surface of the city of Las Vegas when the Moulin Rouge closed unexpectedly in 1955, after a promising beginning. There has always been speculation as to why the dazzling place inexplicably locked its doors for a time; but a specific explanation for the abrupt closing has never really been offered. As the brochure for the 38th birthday celebration of the Moulin Rouge points out: "No logical or acceptable explanation was ever offered for the totally unexpected overnight closing,"[7] when the hotel-casino appeared to be hugely successful on the surface.

Many didn't expect much from the opening of the Moulin Rouge, which was "integrated at all levels, from employees to patrons to entertainers."[8] They thought failure was inevitable, given the underhanded and tremendous pressure from the white owners of the main casinos on the Las Vegas Strip. But their fears about the Moulin Rouge siphoning off business from the Strip proved to be groundless.[9] Moreover, the fear of it becoming some kind of unsavory place because of its racially inclusive showrooms and spectacular entertainment attractions, also proved to be false.

Nonetheless, it became a real challenge for the white owners to keep the place open and running as they speculated about where it was heading. From a purely financial point of view, the Moulin Rouge failed because expenses exceeded earnings. But to those without access to the books the integrated hotel and casino's rapid closing seemed to come out of nowhere.

In the uproar that followed, the black community was outraged, and understandably voiced disappointment and displeasure. Indeed, the first closing was a sort of heresy for the black population. Many thought the closing of the Moulin Rouge was a white conspiracy. The timing of the closing was certainly sudden, but there was no evidence of a conspiracy. Others were indifferent. Yet it was so startling for so many in the black community that they blamed the "opposition from white-owned casinos,"[10] as the major factor for its first closing.

Some other notable reasons cited for the closing of the Moulin Rouge after six months were "skimming," and undercapitalization by the white owners, but this has never been definitively proven. Mismanagement and "pressure from the banks that were holding the mortgage," were also given as some major causes for the 1955 closing.[11] Others believed that the beleaguered place failed, initially, because of financial manipulation and outright theft of casino funds. In addition, some observers have even speculated that the closure of the Moulin Rouge occurred because it was a "victim of its unusual location away from other [Strip] resorts."[12] They blame local casino over-saturation in a city without a viable growth plan. The Riviera, Dunes, New Frontier and Royal Nevada ran into major financial trouble, likewise, in 1955.

Eugene Moehring explains in *Resort City in the Sunbelt* that Will Max Schwartz, the major investor-owner, willingly or unwillingly had "not secured enough financing originally to pay all the building contractors."[13] He cites this as the sole reason the Moulin Rouge folded. We may never know for sure the real reasons why the Moulin Rouge closed after a little over six months of operation, but it left an indelible and lasting impact on the thriving Las Vegas community. For some, however, it was a new low for the city in race relations when some Strip hoteliers questioned the very legitimacy of operating the Moulin Rouge. But at every turn, the legal right for the place to exist was defended by esteemed attorney Tom Foley, who was the legal representative of the famous Moulin Rouge for many years.[14]

Eventually, the place reopened, after two years of almost total disrepair.[15] Fortunately, it had not deteriorated completely. In fact, as tough negotiations continued between the white owners and angry creditors, the Moulin Rouge would reopen with a totally different purpose and aim, perhaps dictated by its location.

The hotel "was leased separately and independently from the rest of the place."[16] But hopes of duplicating the success of the Moulin Rouge's first iteration were doubtful.

The Moulin Rouge was eventually purchased and reopened again in 1957 by Leo Fry, who was owner of the LeRoy Corporation (a development company).[17] Many black Las Vegans thought Fry would bring the place further down, and hinder blacks' chances for civil rights, by not providing jobs to blacks. Many also thought that Fry was unfair and unreasonable when it came to treating black and whites equally. This was true. Fry instituted a policy of charging white clientele less for their drinks.[18] In other words, blacks paid more for their drinks and services at the Moulin Rouge. Therefore, many blacks in the city of Las Vegas felt that the glory days of the place were gone for good. Ironically, "when the [Moulin Rouge] hotel and bar opened" with Leo Fry in charge, it "was closed to [most] blacks."[19]

The disgruntled Leo Fry tried to justify his discriminatory policies, especially of charging higher prices to blacks, who did frequent the Moulin Rouge more often for their drinks and gambling. He said that he "was merely following the lead of other white club and casino owners, who had long condoned racial segregation and price discrimination."[20] But that did not make it right. Perhaps Leo Fry resented being told how to run his casino business; or maybe he just didn't give a damn. Fry, of course, felt that blacks didn't understand the big picture, claiming that the Moulin Rouge was always in the business of making money by any means, "rather than [being] a 'shrine' to racial integration."[21] For some blacks in the city, Fry was a shake-down artist.

In the end, the negative racial perception of Fry decreased the patronage and loyalty of the black community, "which may also have contributed to the casino's financial woes." Blacks no longer "frequented the [Moulin] Rouge, or felt an obligation to support it,"[22] period. In point of fact, blacks in Las Vegas continued to righteously protest against Leo Fry, and the strange, discriminatory goings-on at the Moulin Rouge at that time, causing the continuing decline. And when then–Mayor Oran Gragson and the city commission voted to revoke Fry's liquor license in 1960, and again in 1961 and 1962 over the "outrageous drink-charging incident,"[23] and other lapses in good business judgment, it all but destroyed the resurrection. Many people completely lost faith in Leo Fry. He was seen as a villain by the black community. And when those who made money from their investments in the initially profitable operation didn't reinvest in maintenance and upkeep, it spelled inevitable and eventual doom. How could the Moulin Rouge survive in a very competitive economic and gaming environment, especially with the new buildings and mega-resorts being constructed on the Strip?

For many, it was the beginning of the end of the Moulin Rouge — again. But the fight for black equality was still in its infancy. In fact, things in the city of Las Vegas were becoming increasingly hostile, mostly because of the gross income inequality between black and white Las Vegans and a lack of social services for the black population. But landmark social changes in the city were on the horizon. Segregation cut to the heart of the city's dilemma. If nothing happened to resolve the Jim Crow policies of the day, more racial divisiveness, animosity, and social problems were anticipated.

Although the city fathers often tried to explain away the deplorable situation of blacks, it just didn't wash anymore. And unless something radically changed to improve things such as living conditions for the black population in Las Vegas, many threatened to march and burn the city. Segregation made absolutely no sense to blacks. But city officials and white owners of the magnificent casinos on the Strip were still greatly concerned with potentially altering future plans for the casinos' Strip properties, always with one eye on the ever-present Moulin Rouge, the upstart Westside gaming property on 900 Bonanza Road, where everyone could supposedly go.

The Westside then, as now, is in a strangely impoverished world, in a city of wealth and plenty. But it was where the black population — still mired in poverty — predominantly and unfortunately had to reside, because of de facto and de jure segregation. Black Las Vegans were also hindered by the many racist city policies, which denied them civil rights, equal access, and equal protection under the law, as stipulated in the Fourteenth Amendment to our national Constitution. And their complaints and concerns were met with harsh, inelegant lip service from white politicians and local city officials. Indeed, the city had a poor track record of providing social services for the black population.

Many black people felt no one was listening. But the white power structure wanted to limit angry racial confrontations in the 1960s. Yet many whites also wanted to stop integration dead in its tracks. Maybe a change wasn't in the cards, as it would have been a complete departure from the old, "lily white" ways of doing things in the city. However, under intense pressure from the state government, Governor Grant Sawyer, and local black activists, things would change in Las Vegas for blacks and in the state — for the first time. It was only a matter of time before the hierarchy at the Strip and the racist house of cards would fall flat. But some belligerent whites were still less than enthusiastic. White Las Vegans were not particularly enamored by the notion of integration.

Black Las Vegans were particularly sensitive to the uproar over racial segregation because things were unfolding fast. Blacks were fighting for their constitutional rights and the same opportunities, rights and privileges that whites took for granted. The black population, of course, wanted immediate changes, as many argued that because they were part of the larger Las Vegas community they were absolutely entitled to the same considerations given to the white population. From the Las Vegas Strip, especially after dark, it was probably easy to forget the surrounding, impoverished Westside neighborhood. The white power structure didn't seem to care. Ultimately, it was all about respecting human dignity — at any cost.

The 1960s were a time when the black community was large and thriving, almost monolithic, with several successful black businesses on the Westside. Later, because of integration, as we shall see, the black community was almost devastated by the gradual loss of black businesses on the Westside. All in all, though, the brief closing of the fully integrated Moulin Rouge, "prompted black and white political activists to campaign for the [total] integration of the Las Vegas Strip."[24]

Chapter Six

The Persistence of Cultural, Racial and Religious Barriers

The fight against racism and discrimination in Las Vegas in the late 1950s and early 1960s neared a crossroads. Blacks in the city began to resist the daily inequities of a racially split Las Vegas community, especially in the gaming industry. Las Vegas during the 1940s and 1950s established written and unwritten policies of discrimination against black people in almost every aspect of their lives, but especially in the workplace. As the black population of Las Vegas increased, racism and the prejudicial attitudes of whites toward blacks became more apparent, creating unnecessary barriers to social, political and economic advancement for blacks in the city. As I wrote in an earlier article, "The blatant, widespread discrimination and segregationist attitudes, in both the gaming industry and Las Vegas in general, spread — at least to a small extent — from some of the southern whites who also migrated to the area in search of riches and a better life, bringing with them the racist tenets of the Old South, which excluded blacks entirely from [so-called] genteel society."[1]

Black Las Vegans had a right to expect better treatment than what was meted out by the local white city government, but they were not sufficiently equipped to deal with the racism of the city, nor were they powerful enough to fight back in the late 1950s and early 1960s. Las Vegas was certainly not the cradle of human rights or land of opportunity that many migrating blacks expected and envisioned. Maintaining only menial jobs, many blacks in Las Vegas were barely able to cover basic necessities, as many lived just above or below the poverty line.

When the Moulin Rouge was built, it was seen as a symbol of economic justice for blacks in that it promoted equal opportunity hiring policies for many positions. It would have served the city well to have taken note of blacks' expanding civil rights, but the white power structure in Las Vegas simply ignored part of its budding population. According to the late University of Nevada history professor Hal Rothman, "Las Vegas's deviance prevented it from taking the lead in desegregation — Las Vegas was no one's role model in those days — but the suppleness of a city devoted to pleasure foretold a more malleable future than other places might reasonably anticipate."[2]

The Moulin Rouge improved the living standards of countless black people and white people alike, as race relations continued to slowly improve in Las Vegas, despite the persistence of racial prejudices and discrimination. Indeed, the racial and societal problems in the city of Las Vegas during the 1950s or 1960s would not be solved overnight. But as would later become evident, the Moulin Rouge would become "a meeting place for community leaders, black and white, seeking an end to segregation in Las Vegas."[3] The Moulin Rouge was an exciting development, although some would later come to see the place as "a bizarre kind of historical pornography."[4] Still others saw the Moulin Rouge on Bonanza Road as comparable to the clubs on the main commercial artery of Harlem in New York on 125th Street, during its glory days, and now in its mini-rebirth.[5]

There were many good reasons why the black community in Las Vegas bitterly and openly began to oppose racial segregation. First, blacks in the city were part of the growing Las Vegas community, but were unfortunately ignored. Consequently, blacks in Las Vegas developed their own distinctive culture and ways of life. Second, whites became aware of the developing racial histories in Las Vegas. "During the 1960s, the most tumultuous years of the civil rights struggle, black Americans managed to garner support from a large segment of the white population."[6] Some whites in Las Vegas finally began to appreciate "a special kinship with the black population which they had not felt before."[7]

Many Las Vegans were concerned about the interaction between blacks and whites, and whether they could cooperate peacefully throughout the city, because there was very little racial mixing during the 1950s and early 1960s. Yet prior to these cautious times, especially in 1905, for example, when Las Vegas was first settled, blacks lived, worked, and socialized with white Las Vegans.[8] This social and racial mingling stopped in the 1940s and 1950s, when the racial hatred of whites took firm and total hold in the city. Nevertheless, many felt that if blacks and whites could gamble and be entertained together in Las Vegas, the city's racism would crumble. Still, life in Las Vegas proved intolerable for many blacks. For example, blacks in Las Vegas during this time earned very low wages in hard, thankless, back-breaking service jobs.

Moreover, many blacks continued to live in the poorer neighborhood of West Las Vegas, as they were locked out of other housing in the city. For whatever reasons, the animosity of whites toward blacks in the city of Las Vegas began to boil over. Increasingly, it seemed that blacks were not even considered a part of the larger Las Vegas community, as they existed on the periphery of the city as a whole. But blacks in Las Vegas quickly started to stand up for themselves and resist every attempt by whites in the city to degrade and demean them. As Roosevelt Fitzgerald tells us, "Even though the overwhelming majority of [black] workers came from the South and were accustomed to living and working under segregated conditions, upon their arrival in Las Vegas, they became aware of their own worth and dignity in ways which they had not previously known."[9] Many blacks who moved to the city believed that they would eventually overcome prejudice.

But the very obscurity of blacks in the city allowed whites to shape Las Vegas into the place that *they* wanted. Meanwhile, the black population was being condemned, marginalized, stigmatized and denigrated at every turn. Blacks' major concern should have been how to stand against the overwhelming tides of segregation and discrimination as they refused to be accepted in Las Vegas as second class citizens. Attaining voting rights, economic and political muscle, and ending discrimination and segregation, especially in hotel-casinos, restaurants and other public accommodations, were of primary importance. And many blacks in the ever-changing city immediately began to make their interests and demands fully known. It became commonplace for white Las Vegans to assert that racial segregation barriers were completely down, "for the first time since World War II,"[10] but it was not true.

Many wealthy and powerful whites, including casino Strip bosses, in Las Vegas were insensitive to the social, political and economic woes of blacks in the city until blacks started to voice their displeasure. Still, the odds were not on the side of blacks. But resentment ran high in the black community in Las Vegas. Whites in the city of Las Vegas were not sympathetic to anything that would undermine their power and control. Some might even argue that actions toward blacks in Las Vegas were simply misunderstood. But numerous blacks continued to be banned from white-owned casinos and restaurants on the strip even with the city's changing and evolving policies on integration. As we shall see, moreover, integration would fail "to generate racial equality — in the sense of individual dignity and empowerment — for most [black] Americans."[11]

But for a town that was known as the Mississippi of the West, "even the illusion of social integration, a mixing place where the elites of entertainment could fraternize,"[12] was a remarkable feat in and of itself.

Without a doubt, the church has always played a significant part in the lives of blacks in Las Vegas — even in conjunction with the Moulin Rouge hotel and casino, which catered to many blacks' social needs and entertainment activities. In the face of growing racial confrontations, blacks in Las Vegas "responded by forming a variety of organizations to knit their local community closer together,"[13] such as establishing a loose confederation of black churches. According to James B. McMillan, "The black churches proved to be the key to organizational success." Black "churches were [also] the traditional meeting places for the black community, and provided a convenient forum for disseminating information to large numbers of people."[14] This contact was especially important during the civil rights movement. The black church, therefore, became the primary focus, the focal point, the center for the racial struggles that directly affected the civil rights of blacks in Las Vegas. As professors Mary Frances Berry and John W. Blassingame write, "No other American institution [has done] so much with so little as the black church."[15] They go on to cogently explain that "the black clergy [and black church] in the 1950s pushed the largest mass-based assault on racial oppression in the nation's history. Spurred on by the Rev. Martin Luther King, Jr., black ministers led boycotts and nonviolent disobedience campaigns throughout the country from 1955 until the 1970s."[16]

Civil disobedience spread throughout the nation. And Las Vegas was no exception, as "the seeds of a twentieth-century civil rights revolution led by the clergy had been planted earlier in two features of the black church: its nationalistic and political orientation."[17] The black church within the Las Vegas community successfully supported the work of civil rights by evoking God. Furthermore, black clergy in Las Vegas during the 1950s and 1960s usually blamed the terrible plight of black Americans on "white racism" and economic discrimination. Thus, attendance at black churches during the civil rights movement remained high and transformative, as the dominant group rejected "the idea of African Americans defining themselves."[18] The black church and its liberation theology attempted to give black people purpose in an effort to unlock the mental bonds "resulting from slavery."[19] The black church tried to eliminate the "slave-master" mentality some blacks psychologically embraced.

The black churches throughout West Las Vegas embracing 60 Christian denominations during the 1950s became "the heart and soul of black life, the brick and mortar of black hope."[20] Interestingly, black churchgoers in Las Vegas were "a tempting target for white politicians seeking a block vote."[21] Indeed, these shrewd and calculating politicians often visited black churches before elections, "to meet with ministers and visit with congregants, asking for their political support."[22] But most times, especially on Sunday, black and white churches in Las Vegas were strictly segregated — that is, until some predominantly white protestant churches began to accept black congregants.[23]

Equally important, one particular black church stood out in Las Vegas for its efforts in fighting for the rights of black residents. The Second Baptist Church, the first black Baptist church in the city, played a pivotal role in defining race-relation issues during the 1950s and 1960s.[24] Second Baptist Church in West Las Vegas stood at the forefront of the protest and civil rights movements in Las Vegas, like the widely known Moulin Rouge.

Current view of the famous Second Baptist Church, 500 Madison Avenue, Las Vegas, Nevada (Earnest N. Bracey).

Many black churches assembled collectively to harness the power of faith and community against covert and blatant racial discrimination in Las Vegas. Ultimately, the Baptists and other religious organizations and Christian denominations gave blacks on the Westside a sense of dignity and hope. The black church was considered the social and political framework of the black community in Las Vegas. Blacks in Las Vegas and elsewhere would eventually have "first-class-citizenship status under the law, a constitutional guarantee,"[25] and soon the nation — and world — would know about it, as the message would come from the black churches everywhere in the city.

Chapter Seven

The Desegregation Agreement

Life in Las Vegas was indeed challenging for blacks because of social disparities and racial inequalities. The political process in the city impeded the participation of blacks because the local government deliberately (in some cases) diluted their vote and political power. The idea of equality for black Las Vegans, as you might imagine, was constantly changing too. As Professor Jos C. N. Raadschelders tells us, "Inequalities become more apparent when changes in the social and economic fabric of society appear to be more advantageous for some people than for others."[1] This astute perception by Raadschelders, perhaps, was the crux of the problem with race-relations in Las Vegas during the 1960s.

Achieving equality was not a hopeless task. Nevertheless, blacks in the city were essentially shut out of the political process simply because they were being ignored. Moreover, social and political policies continued to favor whites for positions of political power. The city of Las Vegas in the 1960s would have to deal with simmering racial problems and the ever-present threat of urban violence. The black population had to do something to change their terrible plight, as the racial discrepancies could not be immediately reconciled. Were white Las Vegans simply interested in preserving their lifestyle? Probably.

The misleading diatribe and boorish answers given by the white power structure to blacks complaining about social problems in Las Vegas would no longer work. More to the point, blacks in the city were becoming loud and clear about their deplorable treatment, and what should be done about it. Culturally speaking, the city's near-disregard of the rights of blacks and the failure of the city fathers to invest in social services for all its people was not only unimaginable, it was unforgivable. White politicians' failure to act would have far-reaching, negative consequences for the Las Vegas community, as the social situation in the city was becoming increasingly unsettled.

Some white activists and local residents wanted to do the right thing for the black population, but many were not sure what that was. Consequently, white Las Vegans inflicted much unnecessary pain and humiliation on the black community. It was a nightmare that the black population could not easily escape. Therefore, as professor Mary Frances Berry has written, black and white "togetherness was also challenged by black activists who recognized violence as [another] tactic for achieving their goals and whose thinking was greatly influenced by cultural black nationalism."[2]

The city fathers, given the gaming industry's enormous clout, were also beginning to fear riots, or racial retribution. Many reasoned that racial conflicts between blacks and whites would be inevitable — that is, if *something* wasn't done immediately to assist the black population. So many things were going on. The white power structure wanted to keep things quiet, to bring the black population under control and crack down on dissent, to avoid the disastrous consequences of angry people boldly marching and demonstrating in the streets of Las Vegas. White officials, therefore, were bracing for headaches. In the 1960s, the Moulin Rouge became a sort of symbol for blacks in the segregated city, and later the lifeblood of the black community in Las Vegas, in many respects. The unlikely place certainly had a tremendous effect on the divided city, the state of Nevada and the nation. According to Clarence Ray, "The Moulin Rouge was supposed to be the thing that would connect whites and blacks ... so they'd get used to being with one another."[3]

But Leo Fry, the owner of the Moulin Rouge, continued to infuriate black and white activists by "charging black customers more for their drinks than white customers."[4] Perhaps Fry did not expect the fierce public backlash for his discriminatory activities. When Fry was finally summoned before the city commissioners, he had this to say: "We were trying to discourage the black people from coming [to the Moulin Rouge]. We wanted them [blacks] to stop coming to the place, but it was in that community [the Westside] and we couldn't just turn them down."[5]

Fry's actions and explanations were inexcusable and disgraceful, and when the Moulin Rouge had to close down its major bar operations again, the black community felt blindsided. Nevertheless, "the Moulin Rouge's brief burst of popularity drew national headlines, and the glare of the spotlight helped illuminate the fight to end segregation in Las Vegas."[6] So in many respects, what was happening at the Moulin Rouge was a good thing for the civil rights struggle. Blacks became even more energized and emboldened as the segregation and unequal treatment of black Las Vegans continued unchecked; but even then, racial segregation was being seriously tested in profoundly challenging ways, and under tremendously difficult and contentious circumstances.

Time was of the essence, because a polarizing decision to eliminate segregation would change *everything* in terms of race in the city. For the most part, however, the city fathers initially ignored every opportunity for a change in the Jim Crow policies. Still, there was sound logic behind integrating the hotel-casinos on the Strip, mainly because of the money that was to be made from both black and white clientele.

In the meantime, behind the scenes, some blacks in Las Vegas angrily dismissed what whites were saying about the provocative and divisive issues. Many blacks thought that it all narrowed down to *white racism*, which restricted "individual blacks from achieving positions of status and wealth regardless of their capabilities or competence."[7] Racial inequalities "require a type of legislation" that need to deal "with the consequences of social and economic change"[8] and disparities in a true democracy. Blacks had every right to demand their constitutional rights in the city of Las Vegas. Indeed, what other recourse did the black population have? Acquiescence to white supremacy and dominance?

Blacks were not opposed to physically fighting for what they honestly thought was due to them, as they continuously advocated for civil rights and the prompt elimination of racial inequalities. But, of course, as Berry writes: "The response of the government in its effort to suppress racial disorder ... reflected the tension between the lofty ideals expressed in the documents on which [our] constitutional government is based and the tendency of the white majority to desire summary disposition of those they regard as marginal or powerless."[9]

Although blacks in the city were marginalized to a great extent, some say that it was inevitable that racial changes would happen in Las Vegas. Holding on to racial segregation just didn't make sense. The major players — blacks and whites — were eventually willing to roll up their sleeves and to broker a firm agreement that everyone could live with, which would essentially eliminate city government-enforced racial segregation.

Many of the black leaders of that day were members of the local branch of the NAACP, such as Charles Kellar, Drs. James McMillan and Charles West, the city's first black physician, Eddie Scott, and William H. "Bob" Bailey, later the first black chairman of the Nevada Equal Rights Commission, who made a significant impact on the civil rights movement. Some other important black activists and community leaders during that time included Lubertha Johnson, David Hoggard, Sr., Martha Hillyard, Donald Clark, and Woodrow Wilson. According to the late Nevada governor, Grant Sawyer, all these individuals "were on the same team, working for the same objective,"[10] which was to end racial segregation in Las Vegas, the state of Nevada, and especially on the Las Vegas Strip. Sawyer goes on to state that these black leaders, "each in his own way was very forceful, but while they were not equals in status and influence, and their efforts sometimes followed divergent paths, these men [and women] respected one another."[11]

As the newly elected president of the local NAACP, Dr. James B. McMillan in short order established himself, and became the most outspoken leader for the black community in Las Vegas. It was said that McMillan was, indeed, the real black, no-nonsense power-broker in the ranks of many influential black leaders in the city. Indeed, McMillan help galvanize the civil rights movement and black people for social changes in Las Vegas during the 1960s, 1970s, and 1980s, as he became the unofficial black ombudsman in the city. McMillan, who was born in Mississippi, was able to cut through the city's bureaucracy to report and solve critical racial problems for the black community. But he was also independent-minded and not subordinate to the white power structure.

Many black and white activists said that McMillan could be astoundingly determined, and no one wanted to butt heads with him, as he became the driving force behind racial integration in Las Vegas. McMillan became an activist in an effort to deal primarily with the issues of poverty and discrimination, especially as it affected black people in Las Vegas. McMillan was the right black man at the right time to boost the fortunes of black Las Vegans. He spoke out eloquently for the voiceless, and continuously pushed for racial changes. Noting the difficulties for blacks, because there were still specific racial barriers, the late Dr. McMillan said, "[Las Vegas] was rigidly segregated. You [blacks] couldn't get into any of the places downtown to eat. You could go into [some of] the stores, but if you tried on clothing, you couldn't put it back on the rack; you had to buy it. You couldn't go into any of the gaming joints. The only black people who worked in the hotels were porters, and you couldn't live anywhere other than the West Las Vegas area."[12]

As one can perhaps ascertain from the above narrative, McMillan did not mince any words in telling the white power structure exactly how he felt. And he was undeterred by the failure of the city to do the right thing toward its black citizens, as McMillan wanted to eradicate every vestige of inequality and segregation in Las Vegas. McMillan wanted to put pressure on the city government to eliminate blatant racial discrimination. And with his dogged determination, there were many things he wanted to accomplish after desegregation. As a practical matter, McMillan wanted to show why the treatment of blacks was wrong and how black people were suffering mightily in the city.

Just as significantly, white city officials guardedly acknowledged the disparity of the black community, as the image of Las Vegas, the so-called "hotel capital of the country,"[13] was beginning to worsen. All of this was particularly embarrassing. When McMillan threatened to lead a march on the Las Vegas Strip, he was greeted with derision and disgust by the city fathers. McMillan's life was even threatened by the Ku Klux Klan and the mob for having the audacity to propose a racial march and demonstration on the Las Vegas Strip.[14]

Many white "movers and shakers" and powerful hotel owners in the city deplored blacks in general, considering them disgusting and degenerate, which was far from the truth. Members of the dominant group would have done *anything* to stop such a potentially disruptive march, which many believed would turn off white patrons, the high-rollers and white tourists, perhaps bringing the place to its knees. McMillan tried to check in with everyone he knew who could make a difference. Over a course of several weeks, McMillan even had community meetings in black churches on the Westside such as Second Baptist Church and others to plan strategy and tactics to advance the civil rights agenda.[15] In many respects, he ran his program like a military operation. McMillan once served in the Army as a dentist, and he courted no favors.

McMillan decided to write an inflammatory letter to Las Vegas Mayor Oran Gragson, after consulting with the distinguished Dave Hoggard, one of his trusted lieutenants. He informed the mayor of his intentions. In that 1960 letter McMillan told Gragson, who served as mayor from 1959 to 1975, that he had "received instructions from [the] national headquarters [of the NAACP] to take action against segregation in [the] community." He gave Gragson thirty days to respond, thirty days to tell the black community what Gragson personally would do "to help eliminate discrimination in the city of Las Vegas."[16]

Because of national media coverage about the letter and threat to boycott, the word spread quickly. It was a shrewd and calculated bluff that eventually paid off. But black community leaders were serious about protesting on the Las Vegas Strip. It was then that something very simple and humane happened, when blacks and whites decided to meet to bridge the social divide and address other discrimination concerns. The timing was impeccable. Hank Greenspun, once the owner of the *Las Vegas Sun*, would mediate the long-overdue meeting, called by McMillan as president of the National Association of the Advancement of Colored People to head off a planned boycott and march. According to Woodrow Wilson, Hank Greenspun was invited to attend and mediate because he had the necessary ties to "the power structure, the system, the resort association, the political entity at that time."[17]

The meeting would be held at the Moulin Rouge because of its proximity to downtown and the Las Vegas Strip, and also because of its neutrality. It was not a coincidence that the agreement took place at the controversial hotel-casino. In fact, the publicity surrounding the meeting actually made things go more smoothly, and against long odds. In fairness, nothing nefarious went on during the meeting, or during the negotiations of the historic agreement, nor did the key players have to twist anyone's arm. Nonetheless, the end of segregation agreement in Las Vegas would not have happened without much "hand wringing," especially on the part of white hotel-casino owners and white politicians. Failure of an agreement, moreover, might have led to a perilous fight among blacks and whites in the city. Certainly, any racial progress would have been impeded.

Consequently, the meeting at the Moulin Rouge was encouraging from the outset, despite initial missteps, because it attracted like-minded black and white leaders like James B. McMillan, Woodrow Wilson, Mayor Oran Gragson, Lubertha Johnson, and others, as well as Governor Grant Sawyer and Hank Greenspun, who represented mostly the white power structure and white hotel-owners. Greenspun, of course, had always tried "to bring about unanimity and cooperation with the community"[18] by his hard-biting commentaries in the *Las Vegas Sun* against racial discrimination, which endeared him, in many ways, to the black community.

Meeting at the Moulin Rouge to end segregation on the Las Vegas Strip, March 1960. Dr. James B. McMillan is at the head of the table flanked by Mayor Oran Gragson (left) and Hank Greenspun (right). Woodrow Wilson is seated at the front of table on the left (Earnest N. Bracey).

State leaders like Governor Grant Sawyer tried to foster reconciliation with blacks. Sawyer once told black activists that they had a constitutional right to protest. When asked about the specific rights of the black population in Nevada, Sawyer stated the following: "In 1960 there were a number of sit-ins and demonstration on the Strip, and in the Spring of 1961 the NAACP picketed the capitol to protest continuing discrimination. When the black leadership consulted with me about actions I rarely attempted to dissuade them; in fact, I encouraged them to go ahead and picket. The unyielding, intransigent style of a few powerful [white] legislators made some form of confrontation necessary."[19]

In a way, Governor Grant Sawyer, a white man, was on a sort of crusade to right the wrongs blacks had suffered under the white power structure in Las Vegas and the state of Nevada. Sawyer had a genuine regard for black people that came through in his conversations and his inspiring language. Apparently, Sawyer would have rather seen the desegregation agreement than blood running in the streets of the growing city of Las Vegas. In other words, Sawyer tried to do what was right for *everyone*— all Nevadans; although many black leaders, McMillan included, thought that Sawyer was disingenuous.

McMillan, in his unabashed memoir, *Fighting Back*, made a point of stating that Sawyer even missed the beginning of the famous Moulin Rouge meeting. But in fairness, Sawyer cut short a political meeting in New York to get back to Las Vegas to attend the Moulin Rouge desegregation meeting. McMillan explained Sawyer's involvement in this way: "Governor Grant Sawyer was in Washington talking with the Kennedys or whatever when this damn thing busted in the papers. He got on a plane and flew back here [Las Vegas] quick, and I met with him and told him it had all been settled."[20]

Many blacks in the Las Vegas community waited with bated breath for the final outcome of the meeting at the Moulin Rouge. Some black Las Vegans, however, only watched from the sidelines. The desegregation agreement came after only half a day of discussions — in a matter of several hours. According to Woodrow Wilson, attendees discussed the situation, and "the governor [Sawyer] said he thought that a march" on the Las Vegas Strip "would be detrimental," because Sawyer believed that "there were probably some hotheads and that there might be a [disastrous] confrontation."[21] But many questioned Wilson's recollection of what actually occurred at this important event at the Moulin Rouge. Black civil rights activist Lubertha Johnson recalled:

> There was tension at the Moulin Rouge meeting. Some people were completely silent, and others spoke up. Some of them [white politicians] did not particularly like having to face the situation and change it, but they felt that they really had no choice. Most of the [white] people at the meeting I didn't even know. I didn't know what their attitudes had been before. There were some of them who appeared to me to be slightly unhappy with the situation, before we actually got a chance to observe their attitudes.[22]

For the black leaders that attended, the meeting assailed the racial discriminatory policies of the city. A sort of immediacy lingered in the air. Throughout it all, black Las Vegans maintained a dignified demeanor compared to some of the angry white attendees, who initially scoffed at the idea of complete integration.

Governor Sawyer thought that full desegregation merited serious consideration. But he urged caution. The white politicians thought that things should change incrementally, but that would never do as far as the black leaders were concerned. Contrary to the conventional ideas of the time, McMillan and the other black leaders were not so naïve as to accept the current reality as the only way things were done, especially when conditions in the city for blacks were patently unfair and unequal. According to the late Lubertha Johnson, "Mr. Greenspun was the person who actually carried the discussion, and they [the powers-that-be] met all our demands fully. We were surprised by that, but it happened. It was unbelievable!"[23] It was indeed a bold vision that "discrimination should be discontinued, period"[24] in Las Vegas. Obviously, Greenspun was helpful because he was able to win over the naysayers, but McMillan tells us that the entire agreement had already been "settled by [club-owner and impresario] Oscar Crozier and a handful of powerful hotel owners."[25] McMillan went on to state that the white politicians didn't really play a significant role in eliminating the policy that denied accommodation to blacks in the city of Las Vegas.[26] The good news was that things were finally going to change for blacks. Insidious discrimination would become a thing of the past. Or would it?

Chapter Eight

Hot Times in the City

While it was unclear exactly how a new integration plan would be implemented in the city of Las Vegas, the abrupt agreement at the Moulin Rouge to end the cursed policy of denying blacks accommodations in most hotel-casinos was announced to the public, perhaps to the chagrin of many white casino owners. Many, however, thought that the Moulin Rouge's desegregation agreement was hugely meaningful and useful, as it ushered in "a period before state statutes guaranteeing open accommodation and employment opportunities,"[1] which was remarkable in and of itself.

But for some black Las Vegans, the desegregation agreement did not matter, because they firmly believed that things wouldn't change significantly for the black population. James B. McMillan took it all in stride, because he firmly believed that *any* form of discrimination ran contrary to human norms and common decency. He understood that some black people would still fall through the cracks, and would be worse off than him and other prosperous blacks in the city. Some blacks would continue to struggle.

In terms of the Moulin Rouge agreement, blacks in the Las Vegas community, at first, seemed unsure how exactly to respond. Perhaps some of the white residents were just frightened of change. Many black Las Vegans, however, complied with the new city policy. What was happening in Las Vegas was a reflection of the larger national trends, and the changes made in the city had a direct bearing on the black power and civil rights movements throughout the country. Ultimately, though, you cannot make laws or policies that eliminate inner hatred and prejudices.

Equally important, as the late Stokely Carmichael (or Kwame Toure) and Charles V. Hamilton wrote in their book, *Black Power*, "individual racism may not typify the society, but institutional racism does — with the support of covert, individual attitudes of racism."[2] The institutional racism of Las Vegas was beginning to slowly unravel. But clearly, eliminating legal segregation and other unfair practices did not guarantee equal opportunities for the black residents of Las Vegas. Whites in the city still wield a disproportion of power.

Not surprisingly once the unprecedented desegregation meeting at the Moulin Rouge was over, there was a rush to integrate, and the Las Vegas Strip was desegregated. Up to a point, that is. Nonetheless, the black community had done almost the impossible, improbable though it may have been. That said, it was unfamiliar territory. The mood in the city of Las Vegas seemed to lighten with the desegregation decision, as the political atmosphere had been extremely poisonous. Blacks in Las Vegas were finally and grudgingly allowed into social settings such as the various Strip restaurants and casinos where they once had been completely shut out. They did this without thinking or caring about making white tourists and gaming customers uncomfortable. Perhaps it is hard to feel exactly what the black population must have felt, but it would have been interesting to see the new Las Vegas when the diversity of the city was enhanced racially and, to an extent, socioeconomically.

According to black activist Woodrow Wilson, desegregation in the city of Las Vegas was not ubiquitous, because there were some white-owned businesses and operations that simply did not abide by the desegregation agreement. Nonetheless, it impacted the entire city of Las Vegas. Some black leaders in the community tested the limits of the integration plan, and whether it was working effectively. Woodrow Wilson put it this way: "We appointed groups of three, four, or five to go in each one of the hotels on the Strip downtown. There was only one hotel that we couldn't get in; it was [the now defunct] Sal Sagev. They had their security to prevent blacks from entering. We tried them. We had people to test [whether we could go into the place], but we didn't create a confrontation. We backed off."[3]

Although some members of the conservative white power elite in Las Vegas found the informal directive banning racial discrimination contemptible, many white casino owners saw the desegregation agreement as an opportunity to make more money. Some hotel-casino bosses believed that if *everyone* was allowed to gamble *anywhere* on the Strip — both blacks and whites — they could increase their revenue and profits. In other words, if all went as planned with desegregation, a lot of people, especially wealthy casino investors, would make enormous sums of money because of the potential gaming cash-flow. And after all, making money was ultimately the name of the Las Vegas game. Though, increased revenue was not completely assured. McMillan explained it this way:

> The hotels had settled [on desegregation] because it was good business to settle. They knew that some southerners wouldn't want to gamble at an integrated casino, but they also knew that they needed to make sure that the convention business stayed, and that white people would not boycott Las Vegas. Money moves the world. When [the casino-owners] realized that they weren't going to lose any money, that they might even make more, they were suddenly color blind."[4]

Many of the city's black leaders wanted to push the envelope even further, however, as they condemned the stupefying "hypocrisy" of the city officials' policies in denying the black population their civil rights in the first place. Moreover, the decision to integrate Las Vegas was supposedly pushed on whites without any legal authority. There was certainly widespread criticism of the desegregation initiative by the white population. Perhaps it was as columnist David Brooks writes: "People say that they want to live in diverse integrated communities, but what they really want to do is live in homogenous ones, filled with people like themselves."[5]

Perhaps Brooks reflects the attitudes of white Las Vegans during the 1960s and 1970s, as more racial integration was an unavoidable side effect of hotel-casino desegregation. Was integration a way of co-opting or placating blacks, and black Las Vegans in particular? To be sure, some whites in the city were still deliberately discriminating against minorities during that era. Indeed, some Las Vegas businessmen were highly upset that they would later have to provide equal employment rights to blacks. Some newly-arriving blacks, particularly from the Deep South, began to get lofty ideas about where they might be able to work on the Strip, as doors were finally cracked, but not entirely opened. Some opportunities were gradually and reluctantly provided by whites.

In numerous ways, blacks in the city were better off, but they still had a way to go. "Blacks had left the plantations and farms looking for a better life — better jobs, better schools, better housing, better chances for themselves and for their children. [But] the places they found [like Las Vegas] did not always come up to their expectations — [and] jobs were not always easy to come by."[6] Nevertheless, for a while, it seemed that things could change. The Moulin Rouge agreement helped galvanize public opinion and blacks' efforts to integrate every hotel-casino establishment on the Strip, while continuing to challenge the unjust laws of racial segregation, and the antiquated Jim Crow system. Even more importantly, and perhaps without even knowing it, some of the black and white activists that attended the Moulin Rouge desegregation meeting paved the way for necessary changes and black empowerment in the city of Las Vegas. And for some, it came as no surprise.

But when all was said and done, some felt that not everything in the now-cosmopolitan city of Las Vegas had changed for black people. In fact, despite everything the black community now had going for it, many still struggled to obtain economic equality and racial justice. In the words of black historians, "The economic status of [black] Americans remain[ed] unequal to that of white Americans at every level of income distribution."[7] And although integration made a gradual improvement of conditions for some blacks in the city, it did not improve things for the black community generally. Indeed, the black population continued to face widespread discrimination, particularly in certain casino jobs, like waitress, bartender, pit-boss, and top executive. Blacks were not even given job applications, let alone interviews for many casino positions. In this sense, blacks never deluded themselves, as many knew things would be tough, especially in the job market.

Black and white Las Vegans were still polarized along racial lines.

Blacks still wanted a seat at the proverbial city-government and political table, because government did little, if anything, to support the black population in Las Vegas. It was not an unrealistic expectation. The black community had every right to expect the same tax breaks, resources and social considerations as white residents from the city government. According to journalist Norman Kelley, it was "assumed that the end of state-sanctioned segregation and discrimination would set in motion events that would lead to economic parity between blacks and whites. It did not,"[8] especially for black Las Vegans.

Problems of poverty, unemployment and racism were rampant in the black Las Vegas community during the 1960s and early 1970s. Furthermore, blacks in the city were still being muzzled and marginalized in almost every respect, especially in employment. "Many young blacks [in Las Vegas] had become tired of asking whites for their rights, listening to liberals talk about gradual change, and they became more militant, shouting for 'Black Power.'"[9]

When federal laws were finally enacted to encourage whites to do the right thing toward the black population and potential black casino workers, many continued to resist. According to Professor Annelise Orleck, "Many casino owners fiercely resisted civil rights legislation in Nevada," primarily so that they could deny blacks certain job opportunities, and "only [provide] limited civil rights guarantees."[10] Still the black population showed amazing resilience against this dark and callous landscape — and systematic neglect in Las Vegas.

But initially, the racial barriers to job and political opportunities were not the black community's immediate problem. The greater challenge for black Las Vegans in the 1960s and 1970s was insuring that they and other minorities were not being treated badly, as they had been in the segregated past. In so many words, black Las Vegans had to remain vigilant. But at least now there was a modicum of racial and ethnic diversity in the city. Still, there was always "the notion that black people had to prove themselves to white people."[11]

Moreover, "most Las Vegas blacks, despite the integration of public places, still could not live outside the ghettos, or attend grammar schools in white sections of town, or qualify for more than a menial job in most Strip and downtown resorts."[12] So what exactly could end job discrimination in the city of Las Vegas against blacks? Professor Terry H. Anderson writes:

> Historically, discrimination had been understood to mean deliberate conduct or hostility based on prejudice, some act treating a person unequally because of his/her race, religion, sex, or national origin. Yet as the government passed major civil right legislation most companies did not have a written rule stating "do not hire Negroes," or a policy that mandated that only minorities be employed in the lowest jobs. Most businesses simply did not chance breaking tradition and perhaps irritating their white workers.[13]

But Anderson's explanation does not excuse how Las Vegas blacks were still being treated in the 1970s, in terms of ill-paying jobs, diminishing jobs prospects, segregated neighborhoods, and poor standards of living. The city officials refused to address or face this reality. The government did not honestly address the needs of the black population. Therefore, blacks made "little progress in attaining economic parity with respect to [the] corporate wealth"[14] in Las Vegas. Disparities between blacks and whites persisted almost unabated. In essence, if you had dark skin, you suffered workplace discrimination, as income-level distinctions between blacks and whites in the city were palpable and clearly unfair.

Furthermore, when the effects of integration were measured, and the *viability* of the privately held and integrated Moulin Rouge hotel and casino finally ended, the black community was almost destroyed, even as legal segregation ended throughout the United States. It is unclear whether the steps taken really benefited blacks in the end. Before integration, the black community in Las Vegas took responsibility for its own economic and societal condition. Blacks learned to trust their own instincts rather than rely on some handout from the city. And at that time, the segregated black Westside was a veritable, vibrant community.

The civil rights agenda for integration was a colossal endeavor, but with the onset of integration, many blacks lost their hard-won livelihood. Indeed, the loss of businesses on the Westside was exactly what many in the black community feared. Within the next several years, black bars and clubs continued to lose tremendous amounts of business to the big Strip casinos. To say the least, desegregation was not fair to black businesses in Las Vegas in many respects. And there was definitely a lot of unhappiness among black business owners, as it brought disastrous consequences to their bottom line, for the years and decades that followed. There was no racial reciprocity. White Las Vegans did not frequent black businesses on the Westside.

This could be attributed to the cultural differences of the two major ethnic groups in Las Vegas at the time. Meanwhile, such turns of events became increasingly frustrating to the black community, and the potential rose again for racial violence. It was becoming a discriminatory war of sort for blacks everywhere.

As a consequence, there were bitter complaints of job discrimination galore, which usually fell on the deaf ears of state and local officials. Therefore, black activists had to spearhead another drive to completely revamp their participation in the institutions of political representation.[15] Amid such an ever-changing environment, many blacks were still relegated to the dung heaps of Las Vegas, and still barred at every turn in terms of opportunities. It also seemed that the black population was largely ignored by the local, conservative news organizations. That relationship has always been adversarial.

Many black Las Vegans thought that there should be more intense pressures to eliminate inequality and racial disparities. They were determined to face the challenges and white power structure head on. Keenly attuned to the political dilemma facing black Las Vegans, nevertheless, "some in the [civil rights] movement argued that it was now time to go from protest to politics, eschewing direct action, and building electoral coalitions."[16] According to journalist Norman Kelley, "This was necessary in order to implement the next phase of the ... movement: economic justice."[17] For reasons that are still unclear and probably contradictory, the non-violent civil rights movement caused whites relatively little concern, possibly because the new cultural and business order-of-the-day was still white supremacy in Las Vegas.

Chapter Nine

Blacks Need Not Apply Here

While racial segregation in Las Vegas had been mostly "relegated to the pages of history" by the 1960s, people of all stripes, colors, and walks of life in the 1970s and beyond were now "invited to leave their money on the green-felt tables of major resorts."[1] We must not forget the white community's initial opposition to the incomparable desegregation plan in Las Vegas. Nor should we forget that the notable and integrated Moulin Rouge was not well received by the white population, either. In terms of local wealth, "blacks were the least wealthy of the wealthy, and poor blacks were the poorest of the poor,"[2] especially in the growing city of Las Vegas.

There were some signs that race-relations were gradually changing in Las Vegas; however, the city continued to ignore the real impoverishment, desperation, and degradation of blacks on the Westside, the depressed black district. Some blacks in Las Vegas were still living in a poverty-stricken neighborhood, without basic utilities and amenities, such as air-conditioning in their homes, running water, sewer service or asphalt streets. Indeed, some of the shacks and inferior homes on the Westside in the city were uninhabitable, but black people could not live anywhere else at that time.

Blacks in Las Vegas could not move into better sections of town, the predominantly white neighborhoods, because of carefully contrived, restrictive covenants. Neighborhood associations in the city willingly and tacitly aided these restrictive covenants by serving "as organized extra-legal agencies to keep [black] and white residences separated."[3] Nobel Prize-winning social scientist Gunnar Myrdal wrote:

> When the courts' opposition to segregation laws passed by public bodies became manifest, and there was more migration of [blacks] to cities [like Las Vegas], organized activities on the part of the interested whites became more widespread. The restrictive covenant — an agreement by property owners in a neighborhood not to sell or rent their property to [black] people for a definite period [took firm hold].[4]

The restrictive covenant was especially popular in Las Vegas after the passing of the 1964 Civil Rights Act. The city's arbitrary restrictions, redlining and unfair laws, as well as segregation, which had the potential to include a large swath of different people, affected mostly the black population, as the city fathers mostly ignored the consequences of their actions. The white power structure only harped on superficial, unimportant things when addressing the plight of black Las Vegans. Was it because white city officials just didn't care? Undoubtedly, blacks still didn't have a real voice. Indeed, many blacks in Las Vegas in the late 1970s had no formal jobs, as many were still attached to a de facto segregated world. For a long period of time, the job options for blacks were limited.

For many blacks, even in the 1970s, continued discrimination and prejudice in the city was reminiscent of what a black person experienced growing up in the Deep South.[5] So Las Vegas blacks had to challenge the one-dimensional thinking of racists. The black leaders in Las Vegas, who continued to fight racial discrimination, also pleaded for more aggressive efforts from those in power to improve things for many of the most vulnerable black residents. Some black observers, however, said that it was an exercise in futility to expect the city of Las Vegas to lift a finger to help blacks, without being coerced in some way. The white community, of course, had the power to hurt the black community through redlining and political measures, but their authority and power were not absolute. Equally importantly, blacks in the city continued to be shortchanged in the delivery of public services.

Furthermore, according to journalist Larry Werner, white-owned banks resisted making loans in the predominantly black sections of town by "redlining the area, particularly where existing businesses" desperately needed "loans to expand," and where black people also needed loans to improve their homes.[6] City officials knew that destitute blacks had serious problems, but the white political machine initially chose to ignore these legitimate concerns. Did white officials think that by ignoring such important matters, they would go away? Probably.

It cannot be overstated that the main problem for blacks in Las Vegas was still a lack of job opportunities, which contributed to the frustrations that continued to build up in the black community. The black population, however, was stubborn in the predominantly black West Las Vegas. Werner writes that "centuries of economic repression ... forged a black community well acquainted with survival. [And] historically, much of that will to survive [had] come from the [black] church."[7] It must be understood that "only a *minute* portion of the black community" could even have been "considered a ghetto"[8] in the 1970s. Journalists Harold Hyman and Bob Palm, writing in the *Las Vegas Sun* in 1979 put it this way: "The image that blacks are welfare-prone has been vastly overplayed by the white community because they do not see the $100,000 homes scattered throughout the black community, and the men and women, who maybe do not have the most prestigious jobs in Las Vegas, but work hard and long hours to support themselves and their families."[9]

Giving the black population its rightful due came at a time of fierce debate and non-action among white city officials — and the lingering threat of racial confrontation in Las Vegas. But clearly, it was long past time that the black population was given every consideration. The essential point is that black Las Vegans endured and overcame a misguided attempt by the conservative white power elites to exclude them from the riches of the city. And as bad as things seemed to be for most minorities, they were even worse for blacks in Las Vegas. The deeper truth of the matter is that throughout this time period, the poverty of blacks should have been tackled completely and in a timely manner — that is, by providing decent jobs, feeding hungry black children, and providing public-works projects on the Westside for black Las Vegans.

To do otherwise was an affront by the white power structure to blacks living *anywhere* in the city of Las Vegas. Or was it a calculated effort on the part of the city officials to dismiss the terrible conditions, as well as the trials and tribulations of the black community in Las Vegas? Indeed, "explicit racial discrimination by [white] developers, realtors, banks, government agencies, and individual home buyers revealed the widespread awareness"[10] of the persistence of racism and segmentation in Las Vegas. White neighborhoods in the city "were seen from the beginning as privileged places whose residents were going to do whatever they could to improve the quality of their personal lives at the expense of [some Las Vegans] — that is, people of color."[11]

Black Las Vegans were wrongly and disproportionately affected by the economic inequality and racial exclusivity of the city. Blacks, however, were determined to persevere, despite the explicit racial discrimination. Eventually, in 1975, white city officials "pumped almost $6 million in federal grants into the black community for roads, street lights, sewers, housing rehabilitation and economic development programs."[12] Such services were long overdue. Why did it take so long for white civic officials to do the right thing? Was it because of the callousness of the white political leaders who denied human services and resources to the black community, based on Jim Crow racism? We may never really know why black Las Vegans were treated in such an inhumane manner. But blacks in the city understood their value, and worth.

Another factor was the racially exclusive hiring practices of the major hotel-casinos. The Moulin Rouge, of course, did not play a part in the gaming and hiring decisions made by the casino moguls at that time on the Strip, as the Rouge was insignificant in the 1970s. Nonetheless, in Las Vegas, black leaders continued to negotiate with the white casino owners, to soothe racial tensions in the city. It was cause for optimism. But for some blacks who were seeking parity, decent wages and high-paying hotel-casino jobs, the doors were tightly shut. More trouble ensued when black Las Vegans were denied specific jobs at some Strip casinos. And to add insult to an already bad situation, a suspiciously large number of mostly black males who had already been hired at many of these hotel-casinos were summarily fired for no apparent reason.

It was reported that many of the black males were dismissed because they were dating white women. According to Dr. Charles West, the city's first black physician and another leader in the black community, Strip hotel officials were only trying to "keep blacks from holding a substantial number of key positions," because hotel-casino managers probably didn't like black men dating white women.[13] It was, of course, an emotional powder keg. For Dr. James B. McMillan, who was still president of the Las Vegas NAACP in 1979, and other black activists, throughout the city firing someone for his social life just didn't make much sense.

Civil rights activist Dr. Charles West, the first black physician in Las Vegas, Nevada, 1979 (Nevada State Museum and Historical Society, Las Vegas).

McMillan charged that several hotel-casinos were not living up to the terms of a federal hiring decree in 1973.[14] He also claimed that there were "covert efforts to fire blacks and replace them with members of other minorities,"[15] mostly Hispanics who wouldn't challenge the hotel-casino executives or fight them. McMillan believed that the firings by hotel-casino management were being carried out based on skin color.

The black population felt that Las Vegas was still "inherently a discriminatory town," even with a 1973 mandated consent decree, which was imposed "under pressure from the federal government," where at least 18 Strip hotel-casinos "agreed to hire black employees in 22 job categories."[16] The decree was supposed to be monitored from San Francisco by Jennifer Gee, who was "an attorney in the litigation department of the Federal Equal Employment Opportunity Commission (EEOC)."[17]

Providing meaningful, high-paying jobs for blacks on the Strip, without fear of repercussion because of one's personal life and dating choices, would have made the black community function better in the city. But it was a perennial struggle. The hotel-casino owners should have been more pragmatic in the firing and hiring of black Las Vegans, black males in particular, as the Moulin Rouge did in its 1955 heyday. Black Las Vegans were going through bad experiences on the job in terms of their peace of mind and mental health. Such pernicious social consequences, and "racial disparities on [Las Vegas] social forces," as well as "joblessness, unsafe housing, and other inequities," perhaps, contributed to the anxiety and premature deaths of many blacks in the city.[18]

In the final analysis, Las Vegas Strip hotel-casinos were required to advertise and inform the black community of their commitment to hire blacks, subject to job availability and the applicants' abilities. And perhaps had this commitment been sustained, it would have made all the difference in the world to the lives of black Las Vegans.

Chapter Ten

The Black Political Revolution in Las Vegas

The modern civil rights movement was ushered in nationwide during the 1950s,[1] which unfortunately led to further racial discord, domestic unrest, hostilities and misunderstandings between blacks and whites in the torn city of Las Vegas. Indeed, Las Vegas was being disrupted from within by the pull of contrary ethnic forces. According to noted black civil rights activist Julian Bond: "The words 'civil rights' summon up memories and images in modern minds of grainy television footage of packed mass meetings, firehouses and police dogs, of early–1960s peaceful protestors replaced over time by violent rioters, of soul-stirring oratory and bold actions, of assassination and death."[2]

Bond's accurate description and terse words are important to note because segregation barriers eventually did come down in Las Vegas, mainly because of the activities of concerned individuals involved in the civil rights movement. Although there were wrenching inconsistencies between blacks and whites (on all social and political levels) which indicated a deeper societal problem, the Las Vegas community took its time in solving its abundant racial issues. Were egregious disagreements and dissension between blacks and whites the reason why there were so many flagrant racial quarrels and important differences in the beleaguered city? Probably. Things certainly began to negatively ratchet up in the black community, as many whites in power simply wanted to maintain the race-relations status quo in Las Vegas. From this perspective, many whites thought that the Moulin Rouge, the first integrated hotel-casino, was a misbegotten fluke. But for blacks in the city, the historic place was more than an aberration or a business flop. In fact, for many, the Moulin Rouge was a social and political masterpiece, an architectural and cultural dream come true.

Blacks in Las Vegas acknowledged and grudgingly accepted the dominant order of the local white society, but that did not mean that they liked it. What else could the black community do? After all, blacks in Las Vegas had a profound and underlying distrust of the white community. This mistrust, however, was not necessarily explicit, as there were no overt fights between the fractured ethnic groups until the 1970s. As a general matter, the climate of racial tension continued after racial desegregation, and inequalities remained between blacks and whites. Furthermore, it was widely believed by blacks in Las Vegas that whites in the city were just as distrustful, suspicious, and extremely hostile to the black civil rights movement as before desegregation.

In the 1950s, for example, John and Al Cahlan, white men "who ran the *Las Vegas Review Journal*," the largest newspaper in Nevada, established an editorial policy that "most often reported [about] black people in an unfavorable light, and they never supported black civil rights."[3] Conversely, Hank Greenspun, a white, Jewish man, who helped negotiate the famous desegregation agreement at the Moulin Rouge, "came out solidly" in his *Las Vegas Sun* newspaper, "on the side of civil rights legislation, the NAACP, and desegregation."[4]

It should be pointed out that the Las Vegas branch of the NAACP was instrumental in insuring that social fairness and justice prevailed for blacks in the turbulent city. Indeed, the National Association for the Advancement of Colored People played a vital and important part in the struggle for equality in Las Vegas during the 1960s through the 1990s, a struggle which was marked periodically by violent upheaval. This most famous of civil rights groups certainly influenced public policy toward blacks in Las Vegas. There is a body of contemporary evidence about some contentious civil rights activities in which the NAACP participated in Las Vegas in the 1960s. The late University of Nevada Professor Elmer R. Rusco tells us:

> The Las Vegas branch of the NAACP announced in July 1963, that it would hold a demonstration on the Las Vegas Strip just before a nationally-televised prize fight between Floyd Patterson and Sonny

Liston. A period of intense negotiation, which involved the governor's office and the ERC, followed this announcement. When seven of the major Strip hotels offered to meet with NAACP leaders if no demonstration occurred, the leaders called off the demonstration at the last minute.[5]

Such was the power and influence of the NAACP at that time. Clearly, the local NAACP continuously played a critical role in directing and preventing massive demonstrations by local blacks on the Las Vegas Strip. Even so, the city officials had measures in place "to protect the casino hotels downtown and [on] the Strip from both physical damage and the even greater damage that might be caused by the image of rioters and protesters in their vicinity."[6] But such measures did not stop the verbal clashes, racial brawls and riots to come throughout the city of Las Vegas engineered by blacks because of perceived wrongs, injustices and other festering social problems.

Professor Eugene P. Moehring in his enlightening study of Las Vegas, *Resort City in the Sunbelt*, cites the 1970 racial disturbance at Rancho High School. Moehring asserts that because of several race-related assaults between angry black and white students, "the Rancho riot was the worst single-day school disturbance during the entire civil rights movement in Las Vegas."[7] But we should also consider the peaceful 1971 and 1972 marches on the Las Vegas Strip, led and orchestrated by the unflappable Ruby Duncan and other celebrities such as the Rev. Ralph Abernathy, Sammy Davis, Jr., and the infamous Jane Fonda. Ruby Duncan and her successful Operation Life, a self-help poverty program, were aided by the National Welfare Rights Organization with the two marches on the Strip to protest the state government's abrupt cutting off of welfare checks to mostly poor black welfare mothers. "The [protest] marches on the Strip produced the desired results when, eventually, Nevada reinstated and raised all the grant benefits in 1975. By then, Duncan, who ran unsuccessfully for the Assembly in 1974, was established as a committed community leader and social activist. [Afterward], the entire state began to take notice of this enthusiastic, formidable [and former] black welfare mother."[8]

Ruby Duncan became the driving force for change in Las Vegas

Ruby Duncan (second from left, front row center) and the Reverend Ralph Abernathy (left, front row center) leading activists down the Las Vegas Strip to protest welfare cuts, 1971 (Earnest N. Bracey).

concerning the rights of blacks and status of welfare mothers. Duncan additionally negotiated deals for fairness and equality for not only blacks, but for other minorities as well. Inequity proved to be "another economic problem faced by poorer" people of color in the city.[9] Violence erupted in 1992 near downtown Las Vegas after four white Los Angeles police officers were acquitted for cruelly beating Rodney King, a young black man. White city officials in Las Vegas "blamed the rioting on some of the five thousand young [black] gang members (e.g., the Crips and Bloods) from southern California who had moved into West Las Vegas some time earlier and were simply taking advantage of the Simi Valley verdict to show their muscle and defy authority. Black city officials and

West Las Vegas residents said the rioting was the result of neglect by the city and unwarranted police harassment."[10]

As the population of blacks increased in Las Vegas, their political clout and power grew exponentially. However, the growth of black political power in the 1960s in Las Vegas at first "brought mainly meager rewards at the local and state level — usually token appointments, gradual increases in the number of blacks holding political jobs, and slight improvements in municipal services."[11] According to historian Russell R. Elliott, a significant number of blacks in Las Vegas resided in the predominantly low-income area of West Las Vegas when the census was taken in 1970 and 1980.[12] The black population grew from 24,760 in 1970 to 46,000 in 1980.[13] Blacks are now the second-largest ethnic group in Las Vegas, and have grown to 124,885 according to the 2000 census.[14]

Unfortunately, blacks in Las Vegas today are not as organized as they were in previous years, perhaps because of so many divergent views and interests. Indeed, black Las Vegans now represent a broad ideological and political spectrum. In the past, however, the role of blacks in the city's government was limited, as they remained out of the political loop. Blacks were not eligible to participate, nor were they considered politically significant until the mid-twentieth century. Some in the black community wondered if it was worth the effort to participate politically — underscoring the political problems facing blacks at that time.

But to a limited degree, blacks have been present in the state legislature and local city governments for the past five decades. Indeed, blacks are now a part of a totally changed political climate in Las Vegas. Throughout the United States, black Americans' "political involvement grew noticeably after the 15th Amendment was ratified,"[15] and Las Vegas and the State of Nevada were no exceptions, especially as time went on.

Since blacks were first elected to political office, they have maintained a prominent place in Las Vegas politics. The first black man to serve successfully in the Nevada Assembly was Las Vegan and political activist Woodrow Wilson.[16] The late Woodrow Wilson was elected in 1966, and was noted for enacting the Fair Housing Act of 1971, his greatest achievement, while serving in the state legislature for four terms. Wilson became the model for other black politicians who sought elected office from Las Vegas. In point of fact, almost all of the elected black officials who have served in the state legislature have come predominantly from Las Vegas or Clark County.[17]

Some other prominent blacks who once served in the Nevada legislature include the legendary Joseph "Joe" M. Neal, the first black state senator. Neal was elected in 1972, representing State Senate District 4, and served for over 30 years, until his retirement in 2004. The Rev. Marion Bennett, a local Las Vegas minister, won the first of five terms in the assembly in 1972, "followed by Gene Collins, who won two terms as a Democrat before losing a re-election bid as a Republican."[18] Cranford Crawford was elected to the assembly and served in the state legislature for only a single term before Lonie Chaney unseated him. He served in the Nevada Assembly from 1975 to 1983.

Black businessman Morse Arberry, Jr., was elected to the assembly from District 7 in 1984, and served as chairman of the powerful Ways and Means Committee. After almost 25 years of working for the city of Las Vegas, Arberry left his position in January 2002 as deputy director of neighborhood services to focus on his mortgage broker business. Black Democrat Wendell Williams held the highest assembly position at one time as the speaker pro tem and Education Committee chairman. Wendell Williams won the assembly seat from Gene Collins in 1986. The highest-ranking senate position ever held by a black person was president pro tem, held by Joe Neal, "which meant that he twice held the post of acting governor."[19]

More recent black state legislators elected in 2002 from Las Vegas include Democrats Kelvin Atkinson and William Horne. Furthermore, Cedric Crear was recently elected as the fourth black person to serve on the Board of Regents. In addition, State Senator Steven Horsford, a black man, elected in 2004, was recently selected in 2008, to serve as the youngest minority leader in the Nevada State Senate. These black legislators definitely boosted the political consciousness of the black community in Las Vegas. Blacks also made inroads at the local level. For example, Dr. William Pearson, a dentist, was the first black American to serve two terms on the Las Vegas City Commission. Pearson was succeeded by his one-time political protégé, Yvonne Atkinson-Gates, a black woman and former chairwoman of the Clark County Board of Commissioners. Atkinson-Gates resigned from her position on the commission in 2006 to focus on her various real estate businesses and to pursue her graduate education. Atkinson-Gates was replaced by Lawrence Weekly, a former city employee who had been serving as a city councilman from the newly created Ward 5 when he was appointed to the position by the Las Vegas mayor to serve out Atkinson-Gates's remaining term.

Ricki Y. Barlow, a black man, now serves as the city councilman for Ward 5. He was elected to the position in 2006. Former professional football player Frank Hawkins also served on the Las Vegas City Council (Ward 1) from 1991 to 1995, and later orchestrated the appointment of banker Ken Brass, the second black person to serve on the Las Vegas City Council.[20] Aaron Williams, who served during the same period when Frank Hawkins served as a city councilman, was "the first black member of the North Las Vegas City Council and later the first black elected to county-wide office as a member of the Clark County Commission."[21]

Black women who have served in elected office from Las Vegas include Lynette Boggs-McDonald, who once served as a Republican on the Las Vegas City Council, representing a predominantly "white and Republican planned community in northwestern Las Vegas." Boggs-McDonald, unfortunately, is fighting criminal charges that she lied about not living in the district she once represented. Boggs-McDonald lost her bid for re-election in 2006 because of the residential concerns. In addition, there was June Whitley, the first black woman to serve on the Board of Regents of Nevada's university and community college system. David Phillips, a popular black defense attorney and Ruby Duncan's son, was elected and succeeded Whitley when she retired from the Board of Regents in 1994. Phillips, however, was defeated by Linda Howard, a black business woman, during his 2000 re-election bid. Howard no longer serves on the Board of Regents, as she resigned in 2005 to pursue other business endeavors. Black women also served on the county school board, such as Bernice Moten, a teacher, who defeated the Rev. Leo Johnson for the position in 1972.

Additionally, Virginia Brewster won three terms on the county school board before she unexpectedly resigned.[22] Moreover, Shirley A. Barber, a former principal at Fitzgerald Elementary School, was elected to the School Board (District C) in 1996, after defeating James B. McMillan, who was the first black male to hold the position. Finally, as early as 1960, Helen Lamb Crozier, a black woman from Las Vegas, was elected once to the state board of education, but lost her re-election campaign when it was discovered she was black.

Equally importantly, several black Americans were elected at large and once served on the North Las Vegas City Council. These city council members included William Robinson and John Rhodes, who won outright his North Las Vegas City Council seat but lost his re-election bid. Theron Goynes also served as a North Las Vegas city councilman for over seventeen years, before running an unsuccessful campaign for mayor. Finally, veteran college administrator Thomas Brown served as a councilman in North Las Vegas from 1976 to 1979, until he lost his bid for another term.

Blacks have also served as judges. The late District Judge Addeliar Guy served as the first black district attorney and district court judge in Las Vegas. Moreover, Earle White, Jr., was "elected as a district judge in Las Vegas, Department 4, for two consecutive terms—from 1985 to 1992."[23] Equally notably, Lee Gates, who was elected in 1991 as a district judge, served on the bench until he abruptly resigned in 2007. But the most singular distinction, as far as black jurists are concerned, belongs to Johnnie Rawlinson, who rose "in the late 1990s to become Nevada's first female and black U.S. district judge and Ninth Circuit Court of Appeals Judge."[24] Finally, Michael Douglas was appointed by former Governor Kenny Quinn to the Nevada Supreme Court, after serving as a district judge for many years. Douglas was the first black man to serve at the highest state court level, and was eventually elected after running for the Nevada Supreme Court in 2006.

Black political leaders have carved out an important place in the landscape of Las Vegas. More importantly, they have given blacks a sense of pride and hope for their community in Las Vegas. But as political scientist Katherine Tate has emphasized, "The scope and direction of their involvement in [local] politics in the future will critically depend on the emergence of new [black] leaders ... who [must] prove to be more effective in delivering political programs aimed at achieving the [black] community's long-elusive dream of racial equality."[25]

Tate's astute comments and insights are important to bear in mind here because blacks in Las Vegas have often been concerned with the national political scene, but they are still interested in local and state political issues. Despite the historical difficulties, blacks in Las Vegas have made some progress in the dynamic political arena in Southern Nevada, and will perhaps continue to do so. In the final analysis, says Tate, "Black political leaders [should] continue to advocate [for] renewed federal efforts to combat poverty, [provide social injustice], and [eliminate] unemployment in the black community" in Las Vegas.[26]

Chapter Eleven

The Significance of Black Women in the Civil Rights Movement

Residents of the Las Vegas community should be especially interested in the legacy of black women, who participated up front and behind the scenes in the civil rights movement in the city during the 1950s through the 1990s, and paved the way for progress. Some of these women included Mary Wesley, Lucille Hughes, Mable Hoggard, Lucretia Stevens, Martha Hillyard, Lubertha Johnson and Sarann Knight-Preddy,[1] as well as the great Ruby Duncan and other nameless black women who played a pivotal part in the history and culture of the black community in Las Vegas.

Some of these valiant black women who were pioneers of the civil rights movement had always been a part of the black community, but many were not given the credit that was certainly their due. Indeed, many provided overwhelming insights in ways to move forward with the desegregation efforts in the city. And to a person, these black women were concerned with the ongoing effort to expand the black community's economic and political viability,[2] through means such as addressing the issues of housing, education, and job opportunities, because blacks in the late twentieth century were still not faring much better than they were in the 1950s. And even though Las Vegas was not as segregated or polarized in the 1960s and 1970s as in the past, blacks continued to struggle.

Many of these women, in a sense, gave black activists the moral strength and courage to fight on for their constitutional rights. Indeed, these black women activists wanted to be heard loud and clear, as blacks in Las Vegas had no intention of remaining second-class citizens. Blacks in Las Vegas were finally tired of being preached to by whites. Many were looking unabashedly for a fight. So many of these brave black women were rightly concerned about massive black uprisings and potential violence in the city.

In fact, there had been times in Las Vegas when the black community was desperate enough to take direct and violent action. But a sense of calm and repose took hold during the early protest movement because of the commotion caused by the black women leaders in Las Vegas, especially as many worked strategically with the many black churches on the Westside. Indeed, many black women activists worked things out to almost everyone's satisfaction, which was commendable, given that many started out with almost no resources. They were also early supporters of the women's rights movement, and provided the nurturing necessary for those involved in the local protest movement. Many of their ideas and solutions seemed breathtaking and pragmatic, especially given that blacks in the city were slowly becoming a powerful minority bloc. Furthermore, "with the enactment of the U.S. Civil Rights Act in 1964," black people in Las Vegas seriously "began to emerge as both an economic and political force in Nevada."[3] Nevertheless, some analysts have argued that blacks still lagged behind whites economically in Las Vegas, which wasn't far from the truth, as racial injustices, social injustices, and economic injustices continued, and they were closely tied to the city's history of discrimination toward the black community.

All in all, black women activists in Las Vegas proved to be of considerable value to the various political movements. And perhaps many of these women felt that their specific involvement was more relevant to the consciousness of the black population in Las Vegas than anything else. Who knows exactly? Black women would often take on certain tasks that black men in Las Vegas might have been reluctant to do, like checking to see if white casinos would allow blacks to sit down in their establishments.[4] The black civil right activist Lubertha Johnson once explained that it was easier for black women, because they got along with white people, more so than black men.[5] Johnson goes on to state that black men, more or less, "figured that they might *really* get into trouble—

somebody might get hurt, because the men couldn't afford to back down if they [the white casino bosses] didn't let them in the white establishments."[6] According to black columnist Jill Nelson, "It [was] essential that black women have a loud voice in the [political] dialogue. Without the vibrant participation of black women, black people [were] assured of repeating the same failures that have historically crippled movements for social change. [And] there [could] be no true transformation based on the exclusion or diminution of women's involvement."[7]

Black women's involvement did not diminish. In fact, the voices of black women in Las Vegas, at least for a while, were almost deafening. More importantly, some of these fearless black women made a big impact on the people of the city. But the magnitude of the shock wave for their political activities, initially, was hard to gauge. To say the least, it was very demanding work for these black women activists to rally the black community in Las Vegas. Yet these gifted black women had a very simple job, and that was to help bring about freedom, justice, equality, racial harmony, and concrete political change for blacks in the city of Las Vegas.

Interdicting blacks from politics in Las Vegas from the 1950s and beyond would have been impossible, given that blacks began to flock to the area, mostly from the South. And many blacks were being elected to political office. Many blacks, unfortunately, were massively challenged by the powers-that-be almost every time they asked for their rights and municipal services, or when they went against the white establishment. Many of these strong black women brought to the table an enormous dose of optimism, as things in the great city of Las Vegas were being seen for what they really were. According to a professor of history at Dartmouth College, Annelise Orleck, some of these amazing black women were able to tactfully drag "Nevada [and Las Vegas, in particular] kicking and screaming into the twentieth century, convincing politicians to accept federal poverty programs they had long resisted: the Food Stamp Program, the Women and Infant Children Nutrition Program, and free medical screening for poor children. And they persuaded federal officials to let them administer the programs themselves."[8]

Clearly, these intelligent and dignified black women wanted to have more economic and political power to get things done, as the winds of racial disharmony continued to blow in the dusty sands of Las Vegas. Blacks in Las Vegas still lived on the other side of the opulent tracks, so to speak. However, some of these women activists believed that black people shouldn't have to choose between principle and poverty, particularly in a time of plenty. But the 1970s through the 1980s were dark days for blacks in Las Vegas, given that whites tried to maintain their total grip on power in the community.

No doubt, these were changing and challenging times in Las Vegas for blacks. Many met with resistance when they asked for city services of almost every kind. These activist black women believed wholeheartedly that the city government owed the black population an answer about why they were not receiving certain human services or other government programs. They thought that the city's lackadaisical attitude and measly assistance was a violation of black Las Vegans' rights, and it engendered a deep distrust in the black community. For many, it was also disheartening to think that blacks still had to fight to get *anything* from the city. Indeed, in terms of decent employment, blacks were falling by the wayside.

Moreover, blacks were still being portrayed in an unflattering way by the local conservative media, which was a bad reflection on Las Vegas, and did not portend well in terms of promoting diversity and positive race-relations. Furthermore, the personal faults, human failings, and shortcomings of some black politicians were being used viciously and vindictively against them — sometimes unfairly — by the conservative media, which eventually eliminated their cachet in the black community. Such personal attacks often ruined their changes for re-election to state and city government. Woodrow Wilson, who had been elected to the city council, became one of the first casualties, as he was caught accepting a bribe by a federal sting operation in the 1980s. Wilson later resigned his position as a councilman.

Many black women activists were criticized by white leaders in Las Vegas for their firm positions on civil rights and the like, as well as for their unwavering support for black male politicians. Many of these courageous black women tried hard to interdict the bad press about what was going on in West Las Vegas, and vowed to use every means at their disposal to achieve their political ends. Many were single-minded in their activism — to make things happen for poor black people in the city.

Black women were helpful in mediating a sort of truce between angry whites and blacks in the city. Some had a wealth of practical experience, as well as political influence in the black community of West Las Vegas. For example, when some of the local black politicians were being depicted in the local black media — or in the *Las Vegas Sentinel Voice*, the first viable black newspaper in the city — as being naïve sell-outs for trusting the white city government in the 1970s, black women worked quietly in the background to deflect such insensitive comments. They did this mostly by letter-writing and making heated phone calls to the offending parties. It must have been terribly frustrating for many of these women. The influence of black women in the Las Vegas community can't be underestimated. "Minority groups have achieved both positive and negative results from engaging in alternative forms of political participation. [But] perhaps the most significant success of direct action during the 1960s and 1970s lies in the increased political awareness that minority group movements generated within their *own* communities, as well as among the general population."[9]

Black women supported the building and continuance of the Moulin Rouge hotel and casino in Las Vegas because they honestly believed that it would continue to generate significant gambling revenue for the Westside, as well as support other black businesses. These politically astute black women also thought that the Moulin Rouge would "bring to the forefront" the fact that blacks lived in the city, and that black people helped to build Las Vegas.[10] Some of these black women with economic wherewithal also wanted the towering Moulin Rouge to display its "sophistication" in an effort to go beyond a simple tourist attraction.

Unfortunately, some blacks didn't care if integration or an ambitious plan for reviving the Moulin Rouge would impact their flagging businesses. However, the Moulin Rouge was used "as a meeting place to discuss the Jim Crow policies of city hotels and resorts" in 1960.[11] And black women like Lubertha Johnson were in the midst of the desegregation negotiations, which enabled many to make some sound decisions about how the city should eventually look, and operate.

Perhaps the survivors among these elderly black activist women would be shocked if they saw the Moulin Rouge today, especially considering the controversial and on-going efforts to rebuild the historic place. Some observers today even argue that the idea of re-establishing the Moulin Rouge, which has "an understandable place in the hearts and minds of Las Vegans," is severely flawed because it doesn't take into account that "the area is troubled." They reason that it will take "a lot more than $700 million to revitalize the neighborhood."[12] Nevertheless, black Las Vegas women will still be around when and if the Moulin Rouge is given new life, whatever the social implications or the political repercussions. Indeed, some still feel that the historic place was a worthy acquisition for all its previous owners, and deserves to be revitalized, regardless of the circumstances.

Because of or despite the black protest movement, which some political scholars claim ended in 1972,[13] the "political advances made by [black] women and ethnic minorities, especially in recent years," has increased their chances and "potential for power in politics at both the national and regional levels."[14] Essentially, black women in Las Vegas put themselves in position to take advantage when any opportunity presented itself. And although the city was a waking nightmare of sorts for some blacks, activist black women made a difference in helping poor people in poverty-level jobs. They also helped feed hungry children, and assisted welfare mothers. These black women additionally supported the black men who mostly led the protest movement in Las Vegas, and those who were followers. Furthermore, as the president of Bennett College for Women, Julianne Malveaux, tells us, many black women were "the mothers, daughters, sisters and wives" of black American men who have had "extremely disparate outcomes in our society."[15] Unfortunately, in the past, as today, black men are "more likely to be arrested, less likely to work, more likely to be marginalized, [and] less likely to attend college."[16] But to be sure, black men did not bring many of these social problems on themselves.

Of course, in Las Vegas, as in most of the United States, "black Americans experienced considerable change in their political attitudes during the 1960s and early 1970s,"[17] as black women tried to soothe the anguish, pain and anger many black men were experiencing in the United States, and the city of Las Vegas. Furthermore, West Las Vegas "lost some of the luster it enjoyed during the period of segregation in Las Vegas when black-owned businesses and hot entertainment spots thrived."[18] Perhaps such a place and time will never happen again in the city. Moreover, it remains to be seen if a new breed of black women will step forward and take over the reins of leadership in West Las Vegas, as many of the former black women leaders have retired or died. They are too old to continue the fight for black rights in Las Vegas's poor neighborhoods.

The formidable Ruby Duncan, former president of Operation Life, in her Las Vegas office, 1970 (Earnest N. Bracey).

Finally, understanding these black women, or women of the civil rights movement and black protest movement, should be uniquely cherished in the history of Las Vegas. Indeed, such women as Ruby Duncan and Sarann Knight-Preddy have become iconic figures. These black women and many others were always focused, it seemed, on doing what was necessary for black rights and equality in Las Vegas, especially in getting things done while protecting the human dignity of a people, and shrewdly moving through all the trials and tribulations rendered against blacks, which was endlessly daunting for a time. In the end, their interventions went a long way. Ruby Duncan, for example, remains a charismatic figure, as she was throughout her days as an activist. Therefore, many of these black women in Las Vegas and their political efforts should be recognized and honored with the highest acclaim and praise.

Chapter Twelve

A Lack of Economic Security and Opportunity

Las Vegas, as we know, is the gambling and entertainment capital of the world, and has been booming since the inception of the city and the advent of the casino mega-resort.[1] Indeed, gambling is the "lifeblood" of the renowned city of Las Vegas and the State of Nevada, because "it has turned a wasteland into an oasis."[2] According to the late University of Nevada professor of political science, Albert Cameron Johns: "Gambling is the most important industry in Nevada. It employs thousands of people and earns large dividends for many investors. Furthermore, it has tremendous impact upon the total economy of Nevada, particularly, tourism in its different dimensions, and it is a major source of tax revenues for state and local government."[3]

The significance of these facts should not be overlooked, especially when considering the migration of black Americans from across many of the Southern states, who arrived in Las Vegas in record numbers looking for jobs, and a better life.[4] "Gaming has created [an enormous] influx of new [black] residents into the city and demographers and other experts say [black] people will keep moving here."[5] Therefore, with this great black migration, many black Americans had to find permanent lodgings, because places to stay in the "city of lights" were a rarity in the 1950s and 1960s, particularly for impoverished blacks. Many ended up at the Moulin Rouge, on a temporary basis; but some were able to stay at the historic hotel-casino for decades.

Eventually, a significant population of black Americans settled in the predominantly black Westside in Las Vegas. This is important to note because, as journalist Mickey Kaus observed in his book, *The End of Equality*, "When Southern blacks migrated ... they settled (thanks to segregation) in the African American ghettos,"[6] especially in Las Vegas. This black migration influenced the entire city by "its impact on the nature of black-white social contacts," and influenced "racial segregation in the urban environment, and the transformation of rural blacks into a new [casino-industry] working class."[7]

"A substantial part of the black migration" to Las Vegas can be traced to Tallulah, Louisiana; and Fordyce, Arkansas; and other Southern states. And since the new black residents tended to congregate, they eventually formed a social and later an "influential political force in the black community," which in many respects still exists today."[8] Therefore, we should ask the question whether Las Vegas has ever truly been a transient community with an economy based solely on gaming, or has it been far more settled and residential than many have believed? One thing is for sure: many blacks in the 1960s and 1970s had little chance of moving outside the squalor of the black community or low-income areas.

About such deplorable racial situations, it's been argued that the white power structure really didn't have a guilty conscience regarding the black poverty that stared them right in the face. And although Las Vegas and the State of Nevada "had not officially endorsed Jim Crow policies as some of the states of the Old South had done," whites in the city "had quietly acquiesced in patterns of discrimination that effectively denied black citizens any places of opportunity or dignity in the trade unions or [other] professions." Jim Crow policies in Las Vegas had also "encouraged [blacks] to live in distinct regions ... and had denied them most places of public accommodation and entertainment."[9]

Clearly, as Nevada scholar John M. Findlay, tells us, "the segregation of blacks" in the city of Las Vegas, "and their relatively low standard of living served as a counterpoint to the glitter and prosperity of the gambling capital."[10] Nevertheless, according to Findlay, "the quality of life in Westside started to change in 1955, as banks began to lend money to black homeowners and government agencies invested additional funds for rebuilding the run-down [black] district."[11] Findlay goes on to say, "The coincidental opening of the first interracial hotel, the short-lived Moulin Rouge, indicated a growing interest in black tourists as well. Even greater strides were made ... once Las Vegans realized that their racial policies tarnished the image of the city in the eyes of a country that was increasingly responsive to demands for civil rights."[12]

This thriving black community in Las Vegas of which Findlay speaks had no choice but to survive financially and economically without government help. Nonetheless, for a short period, the black community on the Westside thrived, until, as we have seen, the advent of racial integration. The late black American historian, Roosevelt Fitzgerald emphasized: "As more and more blacks were either directed or drawn to the Westside, marginal businesses began to appear there. Barbers and beauty shops, bars and soda fountains, neighborhood stores and cafes sprang up. All were intended to serve the immediate needs of the growing black community."[13]

At least until the mid–1950s, black Americans and businesses in the poorest areas of the Westside neighborhood were routinely denied financial credit and loans for black businesses and housing by banking institutions.[14] Individual blacks in the city continually had trouble securing personal loans because white-owned banks often resisted making loans in the black district or the Westside. Banks would say that "homes in the [black] district were more crowded and dilapidated, and less valuable and secure than abodes in the [greater Las Vegas] metropolis."[15] Moreover, as late as 1983, the predominantly black Westside still lacked "major lending institutions and shopping centers even though wages generate[d] an estimated $100 million for residents of the area annually."[16]

The inability of black Las Vegans to secure loans can be attributed partially to the lack of employment opportunities. Blacks got only menial and low-paying jobs. And despite Nevada regulations that prohibited job discrimination in hiring, "Strip hotels continued to discriminate against blacks in employment."[17] Unfortunately, as Rusco reminds us, there was an "absence of significant documentation of such discrimination."[18]

Nonetheless, we can surmise that employment discrimination did continue in Las Vegas, because even in 1983, the unemployment rate of blacks had reached an official rate of 15 percent, which, was 50 percent higher than white unemployment.[19] We must also note that it was more difficult for poor blacks to purchase land and homes anywhere in Las Vegas during the late 1950s and early 1960s and even later, because many places were off limits, and local banks and mortgage companies continued their exclusionary policies of not providing "financing for home building on the Westside."[20]

Owning property outside the ghetto during the 1970s would become a reality for some blacks, but local banks continued to discriminate against black Americans when it came to actually lending large sums of money. Focusing on the unfair lending practices of Nevada's major banking institutions, University of Nevada professor of political science Michael W. Bowers writes:

> A 1992 survey by the Las Vegas Alliance for Fair Banking found that only 59 of almost 11,000 loans for home purchases, refinancing, or improvements in the Las Vegas area went to the predominantly African-American Westside. Black families were denied loans 50 percent more often than white families with the same income. Even more significant was the study's finding that black families earning $41,000 per year were more likely to be rejected for home loans than were white families with incomes as low as $27,000.[21]

Apparently, many Las Vegas financial institutions were biased against black Americans, and discriminated against even black, upper-middle class professionals with substantial incomes. This was especially true in the 1950s, and throughout the 1960s and 1970s. Obviously, racism played a role in black Las Vegans not getting loans. "The struggle against discrimination took the form of a search for legislation to prevent individual businesses and realtors from practicing discrimination against blacks"[22] in Las Vegas, and to an extent, legislative policies did work. But such measures still did not help local minority/black entrepreneurs in their efforts to secure financing for starting businesses in and around the Moulin Rouge, or on the Strip.

By the standards of contemporary Las Vegas, blacks had little or no access to many of the "economic opportunities and community resources" that many white residents enjoyed because of the undue influence of "prejudice and parsimony."[23] Nevertheless, as the late civil rights activist and former black politician Woodrow Wilson vividly recalled, "Las Vegas banks [made] some loans to Westside housing, but they [were] not eager, and you [had] to be very lucky to get the kinds of loans that [were] needed in the community ... to refurbish the homes and even to purchase homes."[24]

The city government finally and belatedly infused money into the black Westside community. The city had flatly ignored and neglected the financial woes of black Las Vegans in the past, and "generally discouraged recognition of the problems of minorities."[25] So when the now-defunct Westside Federal Credit Union was created in 1951 in Las Vegas, it was out of necessity. It filled a financial and economic void in the predominantly black Westside and low-income areas, especially in consumer loans or assisting black businesses to secure financing.

Although there were other financial institutions established at this time "to aid black economic development,"[26] like the predominantly black and short-lived Sarah Allen Credit Union (which had to close because of too few patrons), they did not have quite the impact and success of the Westside Federal Credit Union. Indeed, the relationship between the former Westside Credit Union and the Westside community was almost symbiotic because of their proximity to the long-suffering black community. During its existence, the Westside Credit Union tried its best to serve its black customers, who had little money.

This is important to recognize because some community credit unions, as well as small banking institutions, "continue to hold their own, even as the nation's big banks [keep] getting bigger," while buying out smaller banks.[27]

For over four decades, the Westside Federal Credit Union, which was located at 418 West Madison Ave. in Las Vegas, played an integral part in the development of the Westside community. Many blacks who frequented the Moulin Rouge were members of the Westside Federal Credit Union, and felt an almost magical connection to the predominantly black financial institution. The credit union ensured credit accessibility and fairness to the growing black population on the Westside in Las Vegas. Even the late Nevada civil rights activist Lubertha Johnson once invested money that she had scrupulously saved for her notable preschool business, called Operation Independence.[28] About the unique Operation Independence, Lubertha Johnson once stated:

> My preschool is located in the Sierra Nevada Arms housing project. It is called Operation Independence. When the poverty funds came to Las Vegas — or when they were talked about before we actually had them — people came from Washington [D.C.] and different places and talked about the amount of [grant] money that we were going to get. At that time, a very high percentage of people in this area were on welfare, and I thought, well, we'll never be dependent again! It didn't work out that way, but that was my feeling. That's why it was called Operation Independence.[29]

Equally importantly, the Westside Credit Union was once a part of the National Association for the Advancement of Colored People. Johnson even claimed that she had "considerably more than a million dollars"[30] in the Westside Credit Union. Such an amount during the 1960s and 1970s was considerable, incredible, because it gave many black Las Vegans confidence in the minority-owned credit union, which was never a part of a larger banking conglomerate. To be sure, the uniqueness of the Westside Federal Credit Union was that it catered to a predominantly black clientele. Its mission expanded to the entire business community and population of Las Vegas before it closed its doors in the late 1990s.

Of course, the Westside Credit Union started out no bigger than some of the canvas tents and ramshackle homes where many blacks lived and socialized during the early 1950s in the Westside. But the black-owned credit union was largely ignored by the big financial institutions of Las Vegas, and it was viewed with less fondness than other community banks and financial institutions. It was the brainchild of the legendary Woodrow Wilson, who was once the president and later a consultant to the place until he died in 1999. Wilson's business savviness demonstrated that blacks were capable of managing people's money. And unlike others, Wilson, with keen foresight, envisioned the historic institution as a commercial bank.

His hard work and dedication paid off, when he secured financing to begin the place and it was finally incorporated as a little cooperative credit union. About such a daunting challenge, Wilson recalled that:

> I was president of the NAACP, so I asked my board to give me permission to say "members and families of the Las Vegas branch of the NAACP." That's how the Westside Credit Union got tied with the NAACP.... We got our charter in January of 1951, and before the year was out we made a loan. The first loan we made was to a Harold Jackson for twenty dollars. He was paying two or four dollars a month on it. [And] we own the building.[31]

Woodrow Wilson, Republican Nevada state assemblyman, 1967–1971, Clark County (Nevada State Museum and Historical Society).

Essentially, the Westside Credit Union was a non-profit, tax exempt organization, which maintained a modest active membership of 3,000 from an entire range of incomes. This credit union bolstered the black community's economic strength, while it played a formidable and positive role in assisting blacks with small investment capital and savings, and helping them to secure financing, to begin businesses and to benefit from their money, their dividends, and high rates on savings.

So while the larger white financial institutions in Las Vegas were trying to tighten loan standards, the Westside Federal Credit Union did what it could for blacks and other minorities in Las Vegas who had been frustrated over unemployment, low-paying jobs, economic discrimination and grievances over being denied loans. Not surprisingly, the Westside Federal Credit Union eventually helped the black community in Las Vegas prosper, as well as provided a secure place to save their hard-earned money—and to be ultimately welcomed and included. Furthermore, for those black credit union members seeking a home mortgage, or real-estate loans, the Westside Federal Credit Union had a history of minority lending, without credit risk. Indeed, Wilson long gave credence to this assertion:

> The majority of our loans would be Westside property. We have some cut in the outlying areas, but the majority of it is Westside property. We can extend a personal credit. A person can borrow on for providential needs, they can borrow for furniture, automobiles, education — most any type of loan that can be made by the banks or other financial institutions. We are [also] able to make small business loans.[32]

The Westside Federal Credit Union had more than 1.75 million in assets, and the place was once supervised by the National Credit Union Administration, and run by a board of directors of dedicated fellow members, associated with the NAACP. This is important to point out because the NAACP also played a part in keeping the doors open. While the Westside Federal Credit Union was often challenged by economic hardships, it was still a well-run, lean community institution. It had to operate efficiently to survive, especially in the tough years. It finally filled an important niche for the distressed black community of Las Vegas. Thus, the Westside Federal Credit Union also played a minor, but significant role in the history and development of Southern Nevada by encouraging good financial, corporate and investment policies, and advice for loans, in a segment of the community that especially needed them.

The Westside Federal Credit Union easily could have failed. But it did not fail. And under the worst circumstances of racism and financial hardship, it made a difference in the quality of life for many black Americans in Las Vegas. This once-venerable, black financial institution certainly made the economic needs and concerns of the Westside neighborhood known. Unfortunately, there are no predominantly black-owned credit or banking institutions in Las Vegas today.

Finally, the Westside Federal Credit Union showed that in the midst of discrimination, inequality and poverty, there was room and a market for such a viable and specialized credit union in the spirited, but long-abused black community.

Chapter Thirteen

The End of an Era

The next real challenge that confronted blacks in Las Vegas was stopping the decline of black businesses on the Westside. Many of the black nightclubs and hot nightspots, as well as successful mom and pop stores had to close their once-thriving doors after racial desegregation and integration, because of declining patronage. The city of Las Vegas in the 1970s and early 1980s was also still divided along racial lines. Some blacks in Las Vegas were wondering if the commitment to integration was really a mistake. Blacks who stopped frequenting black business operations didn't feel any guilt, as many perhaps thought that there was no longer a need because of integration.

Therefore, with the advent of desegregation, black-owned businesses were inadvertently devastated "on the Westside, and those who had patronized the Moulin Rouge were no longer limited as to where they could go."[1] As late as "the 1980s blacks [in the United States] owned approximately 17 million fewer businesses than whites," which negatively affected black business profits everywhere. And "an additional deficit [was] that black-owned businesses [tended] to be substantially smaller than white-owned ones." This meant that "in identical areas of commerce, black business income [fell] short of that of white businesses."[2]

Every bankrupt business on the Westside was a tremendous loss because of the income disparities and disintegration of the depressed Las Vegas black neighborhood. "It was not a good time for Westside businesses, whose entire livelihoods depended on black [customers], patrons and support."[3] The Moulin Rouge was no exception, as "it suffered greatly and just as much as other area [black] businesses."[4] Things got even worse at the Moulin Rouge under Leo Fry's stringent leadership, who had now operated the place since 1957.

Fry continued to ignore the level of dissatisfaction the black community had for him and his ideological, social, and business parochialism. Fry, as "the principal stock holder of the LeRoy Corporation," was perhaps upset because the income of the Moulin Rouge during his ownership[5] was not what he thought it should have been. Leo Fry was once quoted as saying that the Moulin Rouge was "economically obsolescent," because "the general area and immediate neighborhood [was] socially and economically blighted."[6] Fry had been desperately trying to sell the Moulin Rouge in the early 1960s.[7] He valued the place — the combination hotel-apartments and land, which spread over approximately 8.5 acres at only $948,000.[8]

However, in 1968, a different estimate put the value of the Moulin Rouge at almost $4.8 million.[9] The Moulin Rouge was later offered for sale to the Clark County Commission for use as "an extended care facility of Southern Nevada Memorial Hospital."[10] But the county commission was not interested in buying the place or establishing an extended hospital.

Perhaps, after such disappointments, Leo Fry had had enough of the Moulin Rouge, when in 1968, the Las Vegas city commissioners ordered the closure of the Hideaway Cocktail Lounge there because of "allegations of on-premise prostitution and serving liquor to minors,"[11] as well as other alleged illegal activities. The suspension, however, was later withdrawn, and the Moulin Rouge's liquor license was reinstated by a district court, which eventually ruled that "the commission lacked sufficient evidence to justify the suspension."[12]

A series of unfortunate events continued to occur at the Moulin Rouge. Prior to the 1970s, the place was picketed by the Women's Democratic Club West, a predominantly black political organization. The group charged that "discriminatory treatment had been given to two of its members," when they were forced to leave the hotel's lobby so that "a photograph could be made for an advertising booklet."[13] Leo Fry, of course, denied the allegation of racial bias by the two black women when he made the following statement to the *Review-Journal*: "This is not a matter of discrimination at all. We have many Negro guests, and have always taken Negro guests. This seems to be a personal thing with these two women. The white people asked to move when we were taking pictures did not object at all."[14]

This statement by Fry, however, seemed to contradict his earlier comments about blacks being able to frequent the place. Eventually, the incident was resolved, after more heated demonstrations by the activist women's group, when members of the bi-racial Southern Nevada Human Relations Commission and members of the Nevada Civil Rights Committee and the United States Commission on civil rights met at the Thunderbird Hotel,[15] to decide an appropriate course of action. In the end, Leo Fry and the Moulin Rouge was not held accountable for what had happened to the two black women, even though it was known that the Democratic Women's Club West had every right to be present in the hotel's lobby, because they had rented a meeting room nearby at the place. The women, nonetheless, had fought the good fight, especially when Gwen Weeks, the strong-willed and courageous president of the club, vigorously spoke her considerable mind by claiming that the two black women's treatment "was a gross insult ... [and] contempt of human dignity."[16]

Leo Fry thought that what had happened with the Women's Democratic Club West was nothing more than a simple misunderstanding. However, as owner of the Moulin Rouge, Fry didn't actually jump through any hoops to please the different people and organizations that had serious complaints. Additionally, financial contract obligation issues and bad management at the Moulin Rouge continued. For example, during the pre-dawn hours on July 14, 1966, more than fifty "screaming teenage girls [in their nightclothes] were evacuated from the Moulin Rouge Hotel when a fire broke out," possibly from a cigarette dropped in room 209 by one of the occupants.[17]

Unfortunately, some of the teenage girls from New York and New Jersey who were visiting Las Vegas as part of a tour called Baron One and Baron Two sustained minor injuries, but they were promptly treated by the on-site firemen.[18] Fortunately for Leo Fry, the teenage girls and adult chaperons did not sue him or the Moulin Rouge, possibly because they were actually responsible for the two rooms (209 and 309) being completely gutted. According to journalist John Crow, a spokesman for the hotel management at the Moulin Rouge, Dan Sullivan, scoffed at the fire damage, claiming that it was a small insurance claim and that the hotel could fix the damaged rooms in approximately an hour.[19] The rooms were later repaired, but it took more than just an hour. Indeed, the rooms were unavailable for a little more than a week.

Later, in 1968, a $775,000 damage suit was filed against Fry and the Moulin Rouge, by "the survivors of [an unnamed] guest who drowned in its swimming pool,"[20] because of violations of health department regulations. But it is unclear from the records if the case was ever resolved. At any rate, the Moulin Rouge never paid the $775,000. The City of Las Vegas filed suit against the place in 1976 for approximately $8,703, claiming that the Moulin Rouge had "been understating the revenue received in room taxes."[21] The City of Las Vegas alleged that this occurred between January 1, 1972, and December 31, 1974.[22]

These nail-biting and unexpected events over the years probably grated on Leo Fry's fragile nerves. Perhaps he was also politically and socially frustrated and even fed up with the black community. Who can say exactly? But in fairness, Fry did allow many black activities and social events to take place at the Moulin Rouge, such as weddings, political rallies, bar mitzvahs, parties, dances, and other black community programs. For example, the highly touted campaign rally for Bob Bailey, later the first black executive director of the Nevada Economic Development Commission, was held at the Moulin Rouge in the hotel's Deauville Room when he ran for city commissioner in 1971.[23] Black entertainers George Kirby and Bobby Stevens of the Checkmates and the Treniers even attended and performed at that sensational event.[24] With other black activists and other community members at his side, Bob Bailey held a triumphant and successful political rally, but he did not, in the end, win the election for city commissioner.

This political rally at the Moulin Rouge for Bob Bailey was significant for the black community because leaders and black activists were beginning to find their collective political voices, by running for public office. In 1979, for instance, blacks made up 5.7 percent of the

Nevada population, but blacks only had a 5 percent representation in the state legislature, or "one percent of the available decision-making positions in state government."[25] Without a doubt, such miniscule political representation left a lot to be desired. But blacks in Las Vegas were moving forward.

Also, in the 1970s the indomitable Ruby Duncan, a formidable black woman and political activist in her own right, mother of seven and once a hotel maid and kitchen worker at the Moulin Rouge, created Operation Life, an anti-poverty organization that catered to mostly black and other minority welfare mothers in Nevada. "Duncan started out her operation under the auspices of the [National] Welfare Rights Organization which she chaired in Nevada," in one of the many rooms at the Moulin Rouge Hotel, before moving the set-up to the now-defunct Cove Hotel on the Westside.[26]

Duncan's entire fledgling operation was ordered by hotel management to vacate the Moulin Rouge, even though she was a reliable and paying occupant. But in Duncan's words, she was asked promptly to leave the hotel-apartments by "the white owners at the time, and without a full explanation."[27] Clearly running a controversial political organization such as Operation Life at the Moulin Rouge was not the most strategic thing to do, given the circumstances. But Duncan made do for a time at the place. No doubt Ruby Duncan's ambition, political organization, and helpful activities at the Moulin Rouge were extremely irritating to Leo Fry personally. He probably didn't like the very idea of having black welfare mothers on his premises.

In the end, perhaps the battered Leo Fry was tired of the cutthroat casino business when he finally decided to pick up stakes and leave the Moulin Rouge once and for all. Maybe it was the daily grind of keeping the place operating. Or was it because Leo Fry was unwilling to endure waiting for any eventual improvement, or uptake in revenue. Or perhaps Leo Fry no longer wanted to confront the black community, who continued to challenge and complicate things for him. Then again, it could have been the thought of more lawsuits.

Leo Fry and his brother Karl Fry finally closed up operations at the Moulin Rouge in 1977, as "the big neon signs were turned off for the last time, casino and restaurant equipment was removed and the doors were locked."[28] Columnist Dick Odessky described this as "a sad day for Las Vegas."[29] It became even sadder when "vandals started breaking up the place as it stood vacant and inviting."[30]

Ultimately, the Moulin Rouge was bought from the Fry brothers on November 1, 1977, by Leonard Roy, a Denver, Colorado, businessman and former coal mine owner, and his son Leonard, Jr., who worked for the Ford Motor Company in Los Angeles for 17 years.[31] The Roys initially did not say how much they would pay for the Moulin Rouge, but the 8.5 acre site was appraised by the Clark County assessor's office for a little more than $800,000 at that time.[32] The Roys, no doubt, were enthusiastic about acquiring the famous place, but much had to be done to reopen the Moulin Rouge — again.

Chapter Fourteen

The Power Brokers and a Raw Deal

When Leonard Roy and his son took over the ailing Moulin Rouge in 1977, it was based on a lease-purchase arrangement.[1] However, neither of the two men had *any* experience in operating such a large and complex hotel, or a casino operation. Therefore, the Roys opted "to lease out the casino," since they only felt "content to run the hotel."[2] It seemed appropriate that the Moulin Rouge continue operation, as the place had had several delicious years. The obvious question was whether the Roys could make a go of it. Indeed, what could the Roys possibly do in the short term to make the place a success again?

At one time, the hotel rooms at the fabulous Moulin Rouge were considered luxurious accommodations, as the place was once considered one of the plushest hotel-casinos in Las Vegas. Now the Moulin Rouge was in a state of serious disrepair. Yet "below a few layers of dirt, and grime," the Roys "uncovered one of the soundest buildings ever constructed" in the city, "complete with all copper plumbing and a generally super plant."[3] In fact, with a little paint, soap and water, and hard work, the Roys did a masterful, Herculean job of cleaning up the filthy place for its next reincarnation. For some the reopening of the Moulin Rouge was hardly news. Still, many in the black community were eager to see the place reopen, which they thought would stop its complete demise.

Not everyone was convinced that the Roys could revive the dilapidated Moulin Rouge. Cynical observers even stated that the place had been kept open longer than it should have been. Yet many blacks in Las

Vegas liked the idea of reopening the Moulin Rouge. In fact, it seemed no one in the black community was worried about the new direction the white operators wanted to take. Of course, the late 1970s and early 1980s were still uncomfortable times for blacks in the city of Las Vegas. Black Las Vegans still lived in an almost separate world where there were few opportunities for real advancement, dead-end jobs and low-wage work, especially on the Strip.

Nevertheless, some blacks in the Las Vegas community seemed more willing to accept the Roys' big ideas. But the new owners of the Moulin Rouge never reached out to blacks in the city. Such a considerate move would have put the new white owners in good standing with the black community. Was it because they didn't particularly care? More importantly, was the oversight on their part a mistake, because they needed black support? For a while the new white owner/operators really did think that they could run the Moulin Rouge successfully. They may have believed that the place could endure with harder work — or a bit of luck. Or perhaps the new white owners had unrealistic expectations for the Moulin Rouge.

Needless to say, both men were pragmatic, and under no illusion about their expensive purchase, because they recognized that they were "gambling some pretty heavy money" on a place that had totally beaten others.[4] Indeed, should Leonard Roy and his reliable son have had lower expectations? After all, there was no hard evidence that the Moulin Rouge could ever be a true success. In any case, an opportunity existed for a new revival of the hotel-casino resort. But before the new white owners could reopen, they had to get a liquor license. Indeed, Roy and his son had planned to open the Moulin Rouge on April 1, 1977, but their application for a liquor license had not been approved by the city by then.[5] Meanwhile, the Roys continued to make "necessary improvements to the Moulin Rouge" so that it could again be "habitable for tourists."[6] For some Las Vegas residents it seemed incredible that the place was able to open again at all, it was in such bad shape.

Leonard Roy and his able son said that the new Moulin Rouge facilities would be revamped to include a coffee shop in the hotel, and at least "150 slot machines, in addition to all the other games of chance for which Las Vegas is noted," strategically placed throughout the inside areas, and small casino. Management readied the restaurant, where they hoped sumptuous meals would be "served at the nightly shows."[7] Roy and his son also eyed the 650 seat, palatial showroom, noting that it would eventually book "family entertainment" at "a reasonable price."[8]

Consequently, with almost no advertisement, or "very little promotional effort," and a liquor license, the cleaned-up and improved Moulin Rouge was reopened for business at the end of 1977. It operated with "a respectable rate of occupancy," and many new patrons, while "attracting both group and individual business, similar to the [wealthier] clientele drawn by the downtown" and Strip hotels.[9] It was then that the Moulin Rouge got the Strip hotel-casino bosses' attention — again. People no doubt were still attracted to the Moulin Rouge because it was unique historically. The place still had little problems, as in the past. But most of the new white owners' decision to expand and change the Moulin Rouge for the better might not have been welcome to long-time casino owners on the Las Vegas Strip. For example, when Leonard Roy and his son thought of "adding a 20-story high rise" hotel[10] on the infamous property, some casino bosses balked.

Nonetheless, they never stood in the way of the Roys' plans for building and rejuvenating the place, perhaps knowing that any such endeavor would ultimately fail. The bigger questions were whether the Moulin Rouge could be profitable — and would the place survive? Had Leonard Roy and his son known that failure was in the immediate future, they probably wouldn't have taken on the awesome task of operating the dynamic Moulin Rouge. Incredibly, at least for a while, the place experienced a renaissance of sorts. The hotel-casino would gain jobs, tourist dollars and momentum with the reopening. Eventually, however, the new white owners seemed to hit a brick wall with the Moulin Rouge. The Roys were directly responsible for the many changes and improvements at the resort. Was it all for naught?

It should have been evident that the place had bad luck, or was a daunting challenge to operate. Did things go wrong for Leonard Roy and his son because of their high hopes? Or was it because of their inexperience? For more than three years, the Roy team, father and son, tried to make a go of the Moulin Rouge. But, predictably, the place failed again. The Roys, in the end, decided to give up their lease-purchase arrangement with the Leroy Corporation.

It was then that "the formidable Sarann Knight-Preddy stepped in, together with her husband, Joe Preddy and her son, James Walker, to [save] the Moulin Rouge from further disintegration and perhaps irreparable ruin."[11] It came as a pleasant surprise to the white community in Las Vegas when Sarann Knight-Preddy took over the reins of the remarkable place, as she was considered a very serious business person, very credible. Indeed, Sarann Knight-Preddy "was well known for her outspoken advocacy of building and supporting business development on the Westside."[12] There was, however, a smidgen of surprise on the part of the black community when Sarann Knight-Preddy took over the Moulin Rouge under such extremely difficult circumstances, because some didn't know her intimately. But given her business background, the black population's fears were soon allayed. After all, Sarann Knight-Preddy operated a casino in Hawthorne, Nevada, for seven successful years.[13]

After Sarann Knight-Preddy's return to Las Vegas, she quickly involved herself again in the politics of the Westside community and married Joe Preddy, with whom she bought the popular Rueben's Cocktail Bar, which was later renamed The People's Choice, after extensive renovation.[14] Journalist Kristi Goodwin explained Sarann Knight-Preddy's business experience and return to the city of Las Vegas, "where she [had] been a resident for some 50 years" in this way: "She gained her experience primarily as a [card] dealer within the Westside community. From there she went to another part of Nevada [Hawthorne], bought and operated a casino for seven years, then returned to Las Vegas where she again took up ownership of several clubs as well as a cleaners and a dress shop."[15]

With her outstanding business acumen and "four decades of [gaming] experience," Sarann Knight-Preddy, who is of mixed ancestry including Caucasian, "Spanish, Creek Indian and Black,"[16] was more than qualified to run and operate a large hotel-casino business. As a matter of fact, the fiercely proud and strong-minded Knight-Preddy was the first and only woman of color to receive a gaming license in Nevada, in 1950, and a gambling license for a hotel in Las Vegas.[17] For our purpose, it must be clearly understood that Sarann Knight-Preddy, her husband Joe and the Walker family were people of color.

Sarann Knight-Preddy, the first black owner of the Moulin Rouge, the 1960s (Earnest N. Bracey).

Before taking ownership of the Moulin Rouge in 1985, Knight-Preddy, her husband Joe, and other family members and partners "leased the Club Rouge and Cocktail Bar at the place from the managing operator[s] of the business"[18]— at that time, Leonard Roy and his son. In so doing, they had hoped "to revive a tradition of black entertainment in a night club setting, as well as [institute] the racial harmony reminiscent of the early Moulin Rouge."[19] Unfortunately, the initial success of the Club Rouge did not last. Nevertheless, Sarann Knight-Preddy was excited by the unlimited possibilities of the place, despite limited success because of a lack of participation from the white community and tourists.

Bob Foster, once a partner in the Club Rouge venture, had the following to say about the concerns of blacks, their blighted neighborhood and the problems of integration, economic inequality, and revitalization of the Moulin Rouge resort: "We figured if the whites didn't want to party with us, we'd party with ourselves. And if any whites want to come party with us, they can come and have a good time."[20] It may have been the creative mind of Sarann Knight-Preddy that came up with the vision of the Club Rouge being supported by both the black and white communities which made all the difference in the world. But as all pioneering black entrepreneurs should know, they may originate new concepts like an interracial club in Las Vegas, but often lose "out later to white competitors."[21]

When the entire, unkempt Moulin Rouge was again falling apart, Sarann Knight-Preddy and her family tried to bring the place back to life, with a vision of a potentially flourishing Westside. The popular assumption at this time was that blacks in Las Vegas had always owned the Moulin Rouge, but nothing was further from the truth. Indeed, it was not until "six years later, despite opposition," that Sarann Knight-Preddy was able to take over the struggling Moulin Rouge as the first true black owner in 1989.[22]

Chapter Fifteen

Economic Discrimination and Education

Before further discussing the expanding opportunities of blacks in Las Vegas, we should examine why Leonard Roy and his son failed at the Moulin Rouge hotel and casino. Perhaps the primary reason the Roys failed at the endeavor was because of their lack of experience at operating such a bloated, problematic and convoluted hotel business. Although the Roys were confident in their own abilities and business savvy, perhaps they were unaware of the complexities of running the historic place, and the dynamics of the fragile environment in which they worked. Perhaps the Roys also didn't see operating the Moulin Rouge as a blessing. Some supporters of the historic place have commented that owning the Moulin Rouge should have been a privilege, "given the site's historical importance for blacks in Las Vegas and nationwide,"[1] but maybe it wasn't all that important to the Roys.

The Roys, moreover, might have thought that the Moulin Rouge didn't really mean anything to the black community in Las Vegas. But operating the historic place as just another business was a mistake. Furthermore, the Moulin Rouge lost business, as already discussed, because the Westside was devastated after the advent of integration. Dr. James B. McMillan once explained that "after desegregation, black-owned businesses" in West Las Vegas "suffered great financial loss as blacks began to spend their money in establishments that until then had been closed to them."[2] In fact, the black community struggled economically and psychologically, as black businessmen and business women boarded up and vacated their precious buildings in the black neighborhood. Those black businesses that remained opened in the 1960s, 1970s, and 1980s struggled mightily to stay afloat.

Clearly, many black businesses were unable to take advantage of the opportunities that resulted from the civil rights movement and desegregation. Or did blacks in Las Vegas no longer care about supporting black businesses and commercial operations, as suggested earlier, once racial barriers had been broken? Some scholars blame the success of the black revolution and civil rights movement for dispersing black residents in Las Vegas.[3] The late black civil rights leader, James B. McMillan explained it this way: "Integration was necessary. But if you were [a black] American, you didn't have to live in West Las Vegas now. You didn't have to gamble or dine there [the Westside]. It didn't eliminate all the money or people, but it did damage the economy of that area."[4]

Let us consider this issue more closely. Blacks in Las Vegas fought hard and aggressively argued for racial equality and fairness. Many were able to overcome the odds, but desegregation did some absolutely no good. Indeed, a large number of blacks in Las Vegas were unable "to rise above economic disparities and improve their lives."[5] Unfortunately, because of a confluence of negative activities and unexpected events, blacks in Las Vegas were unable to capitalize on the changes made in the city, to level the playing field for all ethnic groups. Also, it seemed that the white power structure, in many ways, could have cared less about whether things were fair and just for blacks in Las Vegas. Was it because whites always wanted the advantage and upper hand? Probably.

It was certainly a deep insult to the black community, after being ignored for so long, to be suddenly given the opportunity to shop and go anywhere in the city, like the Strip and other downtown properties, yet still be discriminated against in covert ways. Indeed, many blacks were looked upon with contempt and suspicion. Some black residents, nevertheless, had a sense of optimism with all the sudden changes taking place in Las Vegas because of integration. Yet integration was, without a doubt, a terrible thing for some blacks who lost their livelihoods and businesses on the Westside. The black businesses hardest hit were on Jackson Avenue, which was known as the "black Las Vegas Strip" during the 1940s early 1950s in West Las Vegas, where many of the black nightclubs operated.

These small, specialized black clubs and casinos included the Club Alabama, the Cotton Club, and the Green Lantern, which "was supplanted by Club Ebony in 1948."[6] Some other notable black clubs and operations on the Westside included the Brown Derby; the El Morocco, which opened its doors in 1945 on E Street; and the long-defunct Cove Hotel, which was located on D and Jackson Streets, and where many black entertainers ended up staying during the city's segregation years.

The late Joe Louis, the former heavy-weight boxing champion, owned the Cove, "making it one of the few black-owned hotels in Las Vegas" during the 1940s through the 1950s.[7] Unfortunately, the Cove Hotel mysteriously burned down on July 26, 1989. The Moulin Rouge was not immune to what was happening all around. Many black businesses had to close their doors during the 1960s and 1970s because of a lack of serious black patronage and gaming revenues. And it seemed that the Roys were deliberately not paying attention to these developments during their operation of the Moulin Rouge. Did the Roys honestly believe that the Moulin Rouge wouldn't be affected by the drastic and debilitating changes occurring in West Las Vegas because of integration? Or did they know something others did not? Probably not.

Furthermore, many critics believed now what skeptics thought in the past, that the area around the Moulin Rouge hotel and casino was in no position to support such an establishment.[8] Or was the black community being held hostage psychologically by the Roys, as some academicians believe some Moulin Rouge owners did.[9] In the ultimate analysis, Leonard Roy and his son were unprepared or unable to weather the tempestuous storm of change taking place in the Las Vegas community. Perhaps, in the end, the Roys relished the idea of getting out and handing over the reins of the Moulin Rouge to Sarann Knight-Preddy and her family.

According to journalist Clarence Page, "the past teaches us that government can help open up opportunities for the poor to receive jobs, education and training."[10] In Las Vegas, it was important that the black population, the poorest of ethnic groups at that time, get its due, given the city's record of past discrimination. Education was the key to black progress in Las Vegas, but unfortunately, things did not always work out exactly as hoped for the black community, especially regarding education. The biggest challenge that faced blacks in the city during the twentieth century was how to eliminate poverty through education. Indeed, many blacks in Las Vegas began "to direct their efforts towards problems of black poverty rather than towards the lack of legal equality."[11] The late and celebrated economist James K. Galbraith put it this way: "Access to education is a gateway to opportunity in [black] America, and few doubt (in public) that additional years in the classroom are socially useful. Distributing such access across ethnicities and genders [in] a way to achieve some diversity in the higher professions and in political and social elites [is what mattered]."[12]

Galbraith's remarks are especially important when considering the state of blacks in Las Vegas during the 1960s and beyond. Indeed, the participation of blacks in the field of education in Las Vegas has been enormously important. As many black scholars have observed, ensuring that blacks were in total ignorance (even during slavery in America) was just another way of keeping the entire black community under control, as education is a direct link to economic and political power. The powers-that-be wanted blacks to continue to work in terrible, low-paying service jobs. Educating blacks in Las Vegas endangered a system devoted to the preservation of the "backwardness" of blacks, and perpetuation of the dominant white status quo. However, according to professor James W. Hulse, "Nevada had no official statewide policy of segregated schools," even in Las Vegas.[13]

But de facto segregation did exist in the school system in Las Vegas. Indeed, one might be struck by the depth of polarization that existed in the city. But blacks were not necessarily denied an education. Many in the black population educated themselves, overcoming the political odds, even in the midst of several local school crises. For example, in the 1970s:

> A series of riots and disorders occurred at local schools and eventually spilled over to the streets of the Westside. At the peak of the crisis, Governor Paul Laxalt placed the Nevada National Guard on alert. But a series of compromises that provided for the hiring of more black teachers, plus the effective court decisions of Judge Thompson ... allowed the passions to subside without the level of violence that several other cities had experienced.[14]

Race relations in the city of Las Vegas, especially in the local high school system, deteriorated for an extended period. However, few whites spoke out against such a sorry state of affairs. Predominantly black schools in Las Vegas during the late 1960s and 1970s were sorely inadequate. And because of the poverty and blight that existed in these isolated sections of the black community in Las Vegas, many black students were less prepared for an increasingly competitive and complex world. Moreover, the parents of these black students became disillusioned with the white city leaders in educating their children.

In an effort to rectify the inadequate school systems (K-12) and education problems of blacks, the Keller and 6th grade centers were created in the early 1980s. The idea was that black children could achieve at high levels when they were taught at high levels.[15] The Keller and 6th grade centers later disbanded because they simply did not eliminate Las Vegas's worst schools, or the education problems. The Clark County School District later experimented with Edison, at one time the nation's largest for-profit education corporation, especially in the at-risk neighborhoods and minority-dominated communities, but that effort didn't gain any traction.

Black parents in Las Vegas, moreover, protested the move, because they saw Edison as a profit-driven company that wasn't really interested in educating low-income, black kids. To say the least, the endeavor with Edison failed. On the other hand, the Andre Agassi College Preparatory Academy, a $4.1 million charter school, opened in 2001 in West Las Vegas. It was initially established for grades 3 through 5, and expanded through grade 12 in 2008. The purpose of the Agassi Charter School, which is considered a public institution with an open enrollment, is to send all of its students (mostly blacks and other minorities) to college, and "to give them the tools needed to make a better life."[16] Agassi should be commended for his efforts in educating black students in Las Vegas.

For many blacks in Las Vegas, education was and still is a priority, as many realize that education is a long-term investment and commitment to self-improvement and knowledge, as well as a way out of poverty. Indeed, blacks in Las Vegas continue to pressure for improvements in the at-risk neighborhoods where blacks predominately reside. Unfortunately, some inferior educational facilities remain in West Las Vegas. And as far as Las Vegas is concerned, according to Professor Roth Sidel, "The attitudes of policymakers, educators, and students about who [is] worthy of being educated, and about economic entitlement, and the deep-seated attitude about race, class, and gender, also constitute real barriers to educating all the varied groups and individuals within American society."[17]

Unfortunately, for several decades, blacks in Las Vegas had very little influence regarding certain fundamental patterns of education. But there was always a thirst and thrust for education in the black community of Las Vegas. And despite the fact that more schools were being built on the Westside, black parents grew discouraged by the increasing disparities they perceived in trying to educate their children. And when the primary and secondary school system became a target of racial scapegoating and subject to bias, black activists and leaders took immediate action. For example, Dr. James B. McMillan was able to skillfully "negotiate the placement of black teachers in white schools,"[18] while pressing the Clark County School District "to spend more money on assessing the needs of [black] children and on training teachers in proven reading and math methods to increase student achievement."[19]

Moreover, as a member of the Clark County School Board for four years, McMillan "was responsible for ensuring that three new schools were acquired for his district."[20] McMillan once said that he always voted as a school board member, "to get the things [the black population] need[ed] in ... at-risk schools." Ultimately, he went on to insist that the black community must have "good teachers, small classrooms and good buildings,"[21] in order to be successful. Quite understandably, black Las Vegans' path to education has been long and arduous, but black students today do not just attend schools in West Las Vegas; they also attend educational institutions throughout the city. Nevertheless, as the city of Las Vegas has grown, construction of new homes has often resulted in new schools that cater solely to white students. Perhaps this can be considered unintentional discrimination, as fewer blacks in Las Vegas are able to afford or live in these new and predominantly white communities.

Chapter Sixteen

A Dream Deferred Forever

Sarann Knight-Preddy was fascinated with the casino business and it had always been her dream to own the celebrated Moulin Rouge; however, the problems and troubles of the place were immediate, followed by many obstacles she would later face at the establishment "to achieve economic equity and justice."[1] White casino owners would often try to remind Knight-Preddy of what they collectively thought was her proper station in life — essentially the bottom of the casino business totem pole. After all, the local government strongly supported the white casino owners, and the laws became a "major apparatus" for keeping blacks (in Las Vegas and elsewhere) in their so-called place.[2] But the new system of racial equality, legally imposed on the city, was preferable to black Las Vegans than the old ways of racism and discrimination. Desegregation was the right thing to do. Sarann Knight-Preddy understood the bigotry that still went on in the city of Las Vegas, but she didn't let it stop her.

The highly competent Knight-Preddy eventually had to convince Leo Fry and the Leroy Corporation to give her a shot at actually buying the Moulin Rouge. Fry, of course, still owned the property because of the lease-purchase agreement made with Leonard Roy, Sr. Knight-Preddy was able to eventually buy the place from Fry, because Leonard Roy and his son were "declared unsuitable."[3] Moreover, Knight-Preddy finally won the trust and begrudging respect of Leo Fry by shrewdly coming up with the $2 million pricetag, which was also no small effort.[4] Knight-Preddy was able to keep the Club Rouge and Cocktail Bar open, because the city renewed her liquor license — and later gambling license.

Fortunately, Sarann Knight-Preddy would have the expert help of her eldest son, James Walker, who gave up a very lucrative job as a shift supervisor in baccarat on the Strip to support his mother's long-time dream.[5] Indeed, it had been Sarann Knight-Preddy's consummate lifetime goal to own the place when "she first laid eyes on the Moulin Rouge hotel and casino during its construction and attended its opening in 1955."[6] Knight-Preddy's personal experience helped her attain ownership of the Moulin Rouge, such as her time as a young black woman "writing Keno tickets at the Cotton Club on Jackson Street" during the city's segregated years, and becoming the owner of the Lincoln Bar in Hawthorne, Nevada, in 1950,[7] which she operated for seven years.

Also with gaming experience were her new husband, Joe, and her elder son, James Walker, and other family members, like her younger sons Richard and Glen, who were casino dealers.[8] They gave her an enormous boost and often served as great sources of inspiration. In addition, her family provided Knight-Preddy with intelligent suggestions about how to run the troubled place. James Walker was at the forefront of the civil rights movement and integration in Las Vegas. For instance, Walker was the first black firefighter in Clark County, which encompasses the city of Las Vegas, and later "went into gaming like his mother."[9]

After James Walker's successful stint as a firefighter, he began a second successful career as a savvy card "dealer at the Fremont under Ed Torres in the 1960s." Later, with considerable mathematical skill and aplomb, James Walker became "the first black dealer on the strip."[10] Thus, the Walker family's collective experiences demonstrated to the black community and others Sarann Knight-Preddy's progressive, sophisticated thinking. She would never kowtow to anyone, so perhaps her attitude gave her the edge over others who sought the valuable Moulin Rouge property. Although some expected failure, Knight-Preddy never saw things that way, and she gave the place a run for its money. Some might have even said that Knight-Preddy was foreordained to fail at the Moulin Rouge.

The indomitable Knight-Preddy, however, did not pay the naysayers any mind, believing herself in an enviable position. She was also a key figure in the civil rights movement in Las Vegas, as she never lost touch with blacks in the depressed Westside community, or forgot her roots. She remained politically active, even when she left Las Vegas to operate her swanky club in segregated Hawthorne, Nevada. Knight-Preddy allowed black leaders of "the statewide coalition of NAACP branches to use her club in Hawthorne for strategy meetings" during the modern-day civil rights movement in Nevada, because "the El Capitan Casino," a luxurious white-owned resort nearby, refused to accept black customers, even if they had the money for rooms. White owners wouldn't permit any such black organizational meetings at white hotel-casinos.[11]

When she returned to Las Vegas after seven years, Knight-Preddy established and organized the Las Vegas NAACP Women's Auxiliary, proving her political mettle. So confident was Knight-Preddy that she eventually ran for a Las Vegas city commission seat "and was narrowly defeated."[12] Under Knight-Preddy's astute management, things at the Moulin Rouge were beginning to improve. But apparently it was not enough. With empathy for poor blacks in the city, she opened the historic doors wider for some. This might have seemed like a professional misstep, but Knight-Preddy believed that everything would take care of itself. Poor blacks in Las Vegas, because of their growing isolation, continued to face discrimination. Many didn't have jobs and could not pay their way, but Knight-Preddy tried her best to accommodate and help everyone. She also tried through her presence to personally counteract the historical difficulties of the Westside by waking up the very consciousness of the black community. As a consequence, Knight-Preddy's philosophy was come-one, come all. She tried never to turn anyone away.

Knight-Preddy oversaw every detail of operating the Moulin Rouge as she threw herself into the project. Her top priority was to renovate the place from top to bottom, and later build a new Moulin Rouge entirely. Knight-Preddy sincerely believed that the place could "become something other than a cultural artifact,"[13] forgotten in history. For anyone other than Sarann Knight-Preddy and the Walker family, the task ahead might have seemed impossible.

Abandoning the Moulin Rouge at that time would have had far-reaching, negative consequences for the Las Vegas black community, embroiled in its struggle for civil rights. It would have been tantamount to giving up without a fight. An extraordinary amount of attention was given to the place. Many believed that a critical time had arrived in the life of the Moulin Rouge, which still held meaning. This time it would be different. And Sarann Knight-Preddy shared their enthusiasm. However, her woes, and those of the Walker family, had only just begun.

Perhaps the most encouraging aspect of the new Moulin Rouge venture was that *everyone* in Sarann Knight-Preddy's immediate family pitched in to help out, even with a startling decrease in revenue. The Walker family, however, had high hopes, even though the resort would inevitably suffer even more, and even though they had a vision of a better place, and grander things to come. Perhaps just running the Moulin Rouge was all that Sarann Knight-Preddy could handle, even with her level-headed understanding of the casino business. Unfortunately, Knight-Preddy did not have the financial backing she needed to rebuild and redevelop the property.

They seemed to have missed the optimum time to renovate and restore the Moulin Rouge. Of course, for Knight-Preddy and the Walker family, the long-term potential of the place did not help the short-term need for dollars, even after the Moulin Rouge received a $200,000 technical assistance grant in 1992, which was "used for architectural drawings and plans, an audited financial statement, an environmental impact statement, and a marketing plan."[14] This information was needed by the local banks and private sector for a substantial loan to completely renovate "the 110-room hotel and build a complete casino."[15] It would have been interesting to see what might have happened if resources had been devoted to the Moulin Rouge at that time. Journalist Joan Shepard in 1992 explained that the "renovation of the Moulin Rouge would have meant approximately 40–65 new jobs, brought new tourists to West Las Vegas and provided a glamorous focal point and asset to the community, all of which would have been an economic catalyst to the area."[16]

This renovation of the Moulin Rouge about which Shepard writes, however, never occurred, even though James Walker also thought that a newly renovated hotel "in a predominantly black neighborhood would generate 125 to 150 permanent jobs and 50 to 75 temporary construction jobs."[17] Besides the financial considerations, Knight-Preddy had to deal with the riff-raff and homeless that frequented the place. And the black community didn't provide a groundswell of support, even with the newly minted middle-class and wealthy black residents in Las Vegas. All these things exacerbated the situation at the Moulin Rouge. Indeed, at that moment in time, things did not look good for Sarann Knight-Preddy and the Walker family.

The much-ballyhooed reopening of the Moulin Rouge hotel and casino was now a thing of the past. At various times, the place seemed to have been doing okay. But the lack of funds made the strapped Moulin Rouge "financially debilitating."[18] Nonetheless, for eleven years, Sarann Knight-Preddy, her husband Joe and James Walker, who was president of the place, tried to keep the Moulin Rouge "open while trying to find money to restore it to its former glory."[19] Indeed, for several years, James Walker and his bold and unflappable mother did as well as could be expected under the tough circumstances.

Sarann Knight-Preddy helped to organize a nonprofit group called the Moulin Rouge Preservation Association to raise funds for the renovation and restoration project.[20] This certainly was a plus, but it, too, fell short. The support of the Moulin Rouge Preservation Association was not enough to restore the place to its former prominence. Of course, white casino moguls did not give any support to the Moulin Rouge, as they still might have thought of the place as a celebrated nuisance.

Knight-Preddy and James Walker, however, were of the mind that they could get local support and national philanthropic donations if the Moulin Rouge met national historic criteria. The immediate drawback was that the famous hotel-casino was only forty-plus years old, less than the 50-year benchmark for historic designation. With "state landmark status," the Moulin Rouge would have been eligible for state and federal grants.[21] In the end, the Las Vegas City Council designated the Moulin Rouge as a historic landmark, because of the diligence and hard work of Knight-Preddy James Walker, and it was finally placed on the National Register of Historic Places in 1992.[22]

Furthermore, in 1996, the Las Vegas City Council unanimously voted to give the Moulin Rouge "a $3 million loan of federal Housing and Urban Development funds," subject to certain unspecified prerequisites and conditions. This was "the linchpin to getting $2 million more from local banks."[23] Many city residents, however, thought that using taxpayers' money to fund "the 900 West Bonanza Road project" was a bad idea, because the Moulin Rouge was a private business, no matter the community benefits or the "significant historical weight" of the place, or the pressing need from the black owners. The loan was to be temporary with no discretionary use of the funds. In other words, it was not supposed to be a gift to the black owners. In fact, the Las Vegas City Council stipulated the following conditions in approving the $3 million loan guarantee:

- Disclosing all limited partners and how much they would invest in the casino.
- Getting letters of intent from tour companies showing how many people they planned to bring to the hotel each week.
- Capping the salaries of Moulin Rouge operators, James Walker and Joe and Sarann Knight-Preddy for three years.
- Hiring a management firm to oversee the operations of the casino until the $3 million loan was repaid.
- Getting an unlimited gaming license; and
- Getting a $1 million grant from the city's redevelopment agency.[24]

For reasons not altogether explainable, Knight-Preddy, her husband, and her son "accepted most of the patronizing conditions, but objected to a requirement that the casino hire 85 new people and the terms under which the city could start foreclosure proceeding."[25] Things never worked out. The black Moulin Rouge owners were not able to get any significant funds from local banks or private investors to kick-start the renovation project. The local banks and other financial institutions in Las Vegas were, no doubt, "waiting for a signal from the city that the project had merit."[26] But the crucial message did not come in time, adding to the fragile project's difficulties.

Chapter Seventeen

The Beginning of the End

After James Walker, Joe and Sarann Knight-Preddy's fateful attempt to get millions in city funds (in mostly the form of a loan) for renovations, things looked increasingly bleak for the Moulin Rouge, even though they gave it all they had in running and maintaining the place. Knight-Preddy was not beaten or bowed. The black community in Las Vegas was also still solidly behind the black owners of the place. Why the Moulin Rouge did not get the money and support that it needed was a mystery. Was it racism? Were white businessmen afraid of the different social arrangements now in the city? Were they unhappy with black ownership of the Moulin Rouge? Why didn't the local government subsidize the first true renovation and reconstruction of the Moulin Rouge?

Clearly, many blacks were still being left out of the Las Vegas bonanza, and many continued to face stiff odds, because Las Vegas was still struggling with race relations even in 1995. Unfortunately, black entrepreneurs like Sarann Knight-Preddy and her family members had been "no more successful in exploiting the social advantages of blackness"[1] than white entrepreneurs, like the white hotel-casino owners on the Strip who catered to blacks and whites.

The white casino owners on the Strip could have cared less about endorsing the city's deal for the $3 million loan that might have brought the Moulin Rouge some financial relief, as they probably still saw the place as the competition. White casino owners had always been the beneficiaries of policies and entitlements from the city of Las Vegas, so black business people and black entrepreneurs rightfully could have excoriated the local government. Some black members and leaders of the

Black Chamber of Commerce, of which Sarann Knight-Preddy was a founding and charter member,[2] and the NAACP, nonetheless, thought that they were entitled to an explanation about the rejection of city financing for the Moulin Rouge. They never got an acceptable answer. Were Sarann Knight-Preddy and her family members being blackballed in some way? James Walker said that every time they were "very close to doing some things," they had "a way of turning people off,"[3] squelching important financial deals.

It did seem rather strange that they were unable to get any big-time investors behind them. Raising such large sums of money during this crucial time was a big undertaking. In fairness, "several banks and other businesses had come equally close to deals" with the black owners of the Moulin Rouge, though "nothing concrete ever materialized."[4]

Saraan Knight-Preddy and the Walker family's vision of a new, high-rise Moulin Rouge hotel and casino, 1996 (Earnest N. Bracey).

Sarann Knight-Preddy never thought that she would be in financial trouble with her precious Moulin Rouge. Her no-nonsense approach to business, unfortunately, did not necessarily mean she would make a lot of money either. It should have been no surprise that the situation grew worse, even as Knight-Preddy planned to build a 20-plus-story vertical hotel tower and premium casino on the off-Strip property. The black owners envisioned the projected construction having over 500 rooms and approximately 50 suites, as well as parking, retail shops, a lounge, and a bar. In addition, the new structure would have a restaurant, and other outdoor amenities, like a first-class swimming pool.[5] Such incredibly ambitious plans, however, never came to be because the black entrepreneurs failed to get the financing.

Even more importantly, in 1995, the Las Vegas City Council rescinded a $9.5 million Community Development Block Grant loan application from the Moulin Rouge, because the black owners were unable to get a $1.8 million federal grant.[6] The city had made its grant contingent upon the Moulin Rouge getting the federal dollars. The federal grant was denied. But perhaps the City of Las Vegas was really worried that it would "be obligated to pay back the loan through future federal block grant allocations," if it handed over such a large sum to the black owners of the Moulin Rouge.[7] The City of Las Vegas was unwilling to take the risk.

Some believed that the city council only paid lip service to its support for the Moulin Rouge, including seriously exploring other financial options to help renovate the historic hotel resort.[8] Indeed, the city promptly ignored the black owners of the Moulin Rouge and their plea for public help. Was the city council's initial commitment, especially in providing grant money to the Moulin Rouge, false? Perhaps Las Vegas never had any intention of assisting a privately-owned hotel-casino enterprise, even with historic landmark status.

That the City of Las Vegas was unwilling to come up with a workable loan or grant funds to assist the Moulin Rouge was both shameful and ironic, especially given that current Las Vegas Mayor Oscar Goodman recently endorsed a plan and approved funds for renovation of the old downtown post office, at 300 Stewart Avenue, to house a "mob museum."[9] Why couldn't the city find the $6.5 million for the improvement project at the Moulin Rouge when the black owners requested it a decade before? Perhaps we may never know the real answers to these questions, but it is important that we ask them, at least, on racial grounds.

Probably the only ray of hope that Sarann Knight-Preddy had at this juncture in 1996 was when representatives of the Mashantucket Pequot tribe, which owns the highly successful Foxwoods Casino in Ledyard, Connecticut, visited the struggling Moulin Rouge in hopes of entering the highly profitable casino market in Las Vegas and clinching a deal with the black owners.[10] "A number of Mashantucket Pequots are part black" and have always had "a strong sense of loyalty to people of color," according to a contemporary account.[11] Perhaps this sense of allegiance to the black community in Las Vegas was also important because by this time in 1996, blacks had been "unable to take advantage of opportunities that the civil rights movement opened up."[12] Journalist Marian Green described the 1996 visit of the Mashantucket Pequot Indians to the Moulin Rouge: "Tribe representative [were] in discussions with [the black] owners of the Moulin Rouge about investing in the historic casino renovation ... [they] also ... talked to the Las Vegas Paiute Tribe [on] Thursday at a Moulin Rouge cocktail party honoring tribal members who toured the property earlier in the day."[13]

But to the consternation of Sarann Knight-Preddy and James Walker, an actual deal did not pan out. Perhaps the members of the Mashantucket Pequot tribe were frightened away from the place because of its legendary financing woes and poor financial health. Who can say exactly? Knight-Preddy was probably angry with the Pequot tribal representatives at that point, for wasting her valuable time. Frustrated, perhaps she never imagined that things would get worse so quickly.

Knight-Preddy certainly could now grasp the consequences of losing the Moulin Rouge completely. It was a major setback. Disillusionment soon set in, and reverberated throughout Las Vegas, as Knight-Preddy called out to the black community to join her, and assist in rebuilding the beleaguered Moulin Rouge. But there would be no rallying around the black owners, or rescuing the place from its sad predicament. In the meantime, Knight-Preddy thought that the lack of support from the Las Vegas community and private sector meant that she had to be more aggressive and creative with financial management. She went for broke, but it was to no avail.

In the back of her mind, Knight-Preddy perhaps thought that her efforts were for a lost cause. But she didn't grow embittered by the lack of support from the Las Vegas community. Maybe it was Knight-Preddy's zest for living and working in the tough casino business that drove her on to the bitter end? Or perhaps the pressure and enormous stress of the job at the Moulin Rouge became a grind for Knight-Preddy, James Walker, and the rest of her family. Yet they continued to work hard at the place because they ultimately knew what it would mean to fail.

Regrettably, the black owners could not sustain the operation at the Moulin Rouge. It meant that the family would have to give up on its mega resort-casino dream. The turnaround had finally faltered. Some began to blame the owners, saying that Knight-Preddy, husband Joe, and son James Walker failed to take appropriate corrective actions before they finally had to give up on the place. It was also rumored that the owners had a willful disregard for the property and were equally unforthcoming about the real financial problems of the Moulin Rouge. To say the least, many in the black community were disappointed. As one observer stated: "The Moulin Rouge is a magical place.... [And] we need that place for the community, for the black community."[14] But sometimes dreams die softly.

It is hard to say whether the incredible changes Knight-Preddy, Joe, and James Walker had envisioned were possible, even if they miraculously had been able to get financial support. But there was an inevitability about the black owners losing the hard-won place. Some might say that it was inescapable. So what would happen next, as the curtains finally closed for the first black owners?

In the end, there wasn't a lot of fanfare when Knight-Preddy and company eventually sold the financially strapped Moulin Rouge to white businessman Bart Maybie for $3 million in May 1997.[15] Then everything changed — again. It was an amazing reversal of fortune, because the ownership had come full circle with the new white management of the Moulin Rouge. Aware of the financial problems, Maybie liked the location and synchronicity of the Moulin Rouge, nonetheless. Therefore, he bought the 8.5-acre property with the idea of improving it and making money, not necessarily because he cared about the historical significance of the place.

Bart Maybie had a knack for converting rundown properties into profitable business enterprises. Indeed, "renovating depressed properties [had] been Maybie's occupation for 25 years," especially in Las Vegas, for eight years leading up to his purchase of the Moulin Rouge.[16] Perhaps for anyone else the place would have been a nightmare. But Maybie had the time and energy to effectively run the Moulin Rouge. Indeed, the possibilities were endless, as he understood success. Purchasing the Moulin Rouge made perfect economic sense to him, but the historic place was a tough flagship to steer on shaky historical grounds.

He saw great potential in the rundown buildings, and he would later suggest worthwhile improvements. But acquiring the Moulin Rouge was a public relations problem. Black Las Vegans were angry, bitter, and cynical about another white owner of the Moulin Rouge. Although Maybie was no stranger to controversy, he was greeted with skepticism. Blacks in Las Vegas still felt resentment about the continuing income inequality in the city and white dominance. Indeed, blacks were still struggling to rise from obscurity and poverty. Still, the attitudes of whites were improving in Las Vegas, with few exceptions. But blacks in the city had never been satisfied, so that was the rub.

The city was still unwilling to fully "face the racial divisions and economic inequalities that ran [rampant] through" the black community.[17] Although Maybie was concerned about the black population and wanted respect, he wasn't worried about the rash of criticism being leveled at him. Maybie thought he could reach out to the black community in Las Vegas without any misunderstandings if he reopened the ragtag Moulin Rouge again, "as the foot-stomping, toe-tapping club that the pictures on its ballroom walls depict[ed]."[18]

But clearly, it remained to be seen if Bart Maybie could bring back the magic of a previous incarnation, because the Moulin Rouge in 1997 was a physical disaster. Some in the black community doubted that Maybie would reflect the Moulin Rouge's charm, but they wanted to believe in him and believe him to be tolerant of other people's views about the place. Bart Maybie had to work in earnest to show that the Moulin Rouge had true potential.

Chapter Eighteen

The Walls Come Tumbling Down

Sarann Knight-Preddy and her family, the first black owners of the Moulin Rouge, had put together several viable proposals for financing and using city funds, private donations and/or federal grants. But despite all their efforts, they were unsuccessful in getting any public funds for the rebuilding project, even though the place was recognized as a national landmark, and placed on the National Register of Historic Places. Therefore, the Moulin Rouge remained in dire straits.

Some have argued that the Moulin Rouge was a private venture, which sealed its fate in terms of financing. It certainly failed and dashed the hopes and dreams of Sarann Knight-Preddy.

It was an exacting time for the entire black community in Las Vegas, and misconceptions and rumors about what was going to happen to the Moulin Rouge remained rampart. Black ownership of hotel-casinos in Las Vegas was still considered a little bit unusual. It was, no doubt, a sad commentary on where the city of Las Vegas stood on race-relations. As we have seen, "racial protest and racial laws begat more protest and more laws,"[1] especially in the city of Las Vegas. But non-violent black protest and racial laws, as political scientist Joseph N. Crowley writes, "were healthy developments if for no other reason than that they forced society and government," as well as the city of Las Vegas, "to face up increasingly to the American dilemma of the harsh reality of bigotry and persistent, pervasive discrimination."[2]

One must question whether Las Vegas had learned anything. It was hard for the city to rectify some of the inequalities, which to a large extent, white city leaders and officials created in the black community.

But the City of Las Vegas had an obligation to fix things for the black population, no matter the cost. Indeed, as we have seen, the city was once notorious for its lack of services to blacks. And this is still the case today with the homeless in Las Vegas. Nevertheless, blacks in the city continued to face persistent stereotyping, even while many made significant gains, professionally and politically.

The equal and civil rights movements supposedly provided equality of opportunity and integration displaced Jim Crow racism and the terrible era of segregation in the city of Las Vegas. But blacks in the city continue to tackle discrimination. The late Nevada historian James W. Hulse wrote that, "although substantial progress" was made in terms of race relations in the state, "many remnants of the backward policy of the 1950s" remain, which has resulted in blacks having poor educational opportunities, "chronically higher" unemployment rates, limited "employment opportunities and incomes below the average level for Caucasian workers."[3] It is still a very unfortunate situation for some blacks residing in Las Vegas and in the state.

When the hard-charging Canadian Bart Maybie, president of CBC Financial Corporation, bought the Moulin Rouge, he saw obvious financial advantages. Curiosity about the historic Moulin Rouge had always overshadowed the harsh reality for Maybie. The hotel-casino offered him the opportunity to develop good relationships with the local black residents, providing a sort of seamless integration with the black population. It was not Maybie's intent to segregate his new business along racial lines. He certainly didn't want to ruffle any feathers in the black community.

Maybie's robust willingness to take on the place at all was a small miracle. Maybie believed that the revamped hotel-casino could be successful and a thing of beauty. It certainly needed some updating which he would provide. Of course, maintenance of the old place over the years had been extremely spotty, and neglect had taken its ugly toll. Maybie wanted an upscaled place which would look more substantial. Bart Maybie also wanted the Moulin Rouge to be an exciting stomping ground for black high rollers. But perhaps refurbishing the old place was not the answer, given that the old, 40,000-square-foot hotel-casino was, by then, outdated and substandard, compared to others. This might have renewed concerns about the worsening of the neglected establishment.

And although Maybie was optimistic about his acquisition of the Moulin Rouge, it wasn't producing much revenue with its casino, snack bar, and hotel. Could the confounded place produce more income? The Moulin Rouge might have been a financial drain on the new Canadian owner, and perhaps placed a burden on the surrounding economy. But Maybie had a plan. He was optimistic, remarking in 1997 that he had already pumped approximately $3 million "into the buildings, doing painting, electrical repairs, asbestos removal, and ceiling and floor work."[4]

Bart Maybie learned that it was not only going to take additional

The Desert Breeze Apartments on West Bonanza, Las Vegas, Nevada, 2007. Purchased by Bart Maybie as part of the Moulin Rouge Hotel (Earnest N. Bracey).

funds to rebuild the place, but owning the surrounding land and buildings in the neighborhood was critical to sustaining any growth, barring any other problems or setbacks. Maybie later bought "the adjacent Desert Breeze Apartments and a business complex next to the casino"[5] for further development. He also explored other possibilities to restructure the historic place. For example, Maybie "submitted an offer to the City of Las Vegas and the federal Department of Housing and Urban Development to buy boarded-up apartments behind the Moulin Rouge."[6]

Bart Maybie certainly had a comprehensive plan for salvaging the site. But the Moulin Rouge was in an awkward place to begin with. The property is too far removed from the high-end hotel-casinos and important tourist areas on the Strip. Maybie was always asking what could be done to attract investors and businesses to the depressed black area. How could he create profitability at the Moulin Rouge? Indeed, what exactly could be the magic formula for a complete recovery? Revenue continued to decline.

As Maybie was energetically trying to expand the historic hotel-casino, many said that they didn't think there would be a lot of interest in the Moulin Rouge again. Maybie also embraced Sarann Knight-Preddy's plan to develop a condo-like complex on the grounds, as high-rise hotel-casinos were becoming increasingly in vogue in the city, and not just on the Las Vegas Strip. Maybie also felt that landscaping enhancements could provide needed aesthetic improvements to the land and property. Such changes made absolute sense. Still, the Moulin Rouge suffered economically, which was the more immediate problem.

The black community wondered about Maybie's vision for the Moulin Rouge, and his impact on the black community. Some thought that Maybie had questionable expertise as a property manager-developer, but with outright enthusiasm, Maybie and John Edmond (his business partner), really wanted to turn the Moulin Rouge "back into a [sort of jazz-flavor] casino that would house eight to 10 gaming tables and 165 to 170 slot machines."[7] Bart Maybie instinctively knew that there was more money to be gained if the place was in prime condition. John Edmond was even willing to spend over $2 million in refurbishing and furnishing the various buildings with modern equipment.[8]

Maybie and Edmond likely wanted to restore "the showroom back to its original state and create the restaurant back to what it was," providing something unique, like a "Cajun-style restaurant," geared toward both the black and white communities in Las Vegas.[9] The two white businessmen were fully confident, as they both understood the incredible potential of the entire Moulin Rouge property. Maybie further understood that financial success didn't just happen. Someone had to call the shots. So how could the place be revived? Would it also have longevity? And would it eventually be a profitable venture? Although Bart Maybie didn't know exactly when the upgrading of the Moulin Rouge would be finished, he estimated a grand reopening at the end of 1998, or later. Indeed, Maybie believed that nothing would be gained by announcing a more definitive reopening date.

But despite the many important renovation arrangements, Maybie and Edmond did not explain exactly how they would later bring in the crowds, the tourists, the interested customers, as *everything* was purely speculative. Nonetheless, Edmond believed that the Moulin Rouge could "become a major draw in the entertainment business, showing national and local talent,"[10] if they did things right. Yet many questioned whether what Maybie was contemplating was the right approach for the Moulin Rouge, considering its history. A comparison between Maybie and Sarann Knight-Preddy was inevitable.

Knight-Preddy and her family had wanted to open up a workable historical museum of sorts, and a gift shop on the premises, through the auspices of the non-profit Moulin Rouge Preservation Association. The museum would have reflected the decisive role of black Las Vegans, "who were instrumental in the social reconstruction" of the city.[11] Had the Moulin Rouge Museum and Hall of Fame been built, it would have vividly displayed the artistic and cultural works of blacks in Las Vegas, especially in terms of their endeavors in education, politics, and the "social development" of black Las Vegans.[12] The idea was also to allow visitors to buy historical items and selective memorabilia, to bring in some extra income through voluminous sales. Requests for donations might have helped to construct the permanent museum on the property grounds.

To be sure, emphasizing the Moulin Rouge's storied past could have been the answer to its financial dilemma. Maybie and Edmond were not really focused on such matters initially, but would come on board later and fully by supporting Katherine Duncan, who became the director and "the founder and board member of the Moulin Rouge Museum and Cultural Center,"[13] a later version of Sarann Knight-Preddy's Museum and Hall of Fame vision. Duncan was the property manager of the Moulin Rouge when it was undergoing some minor building renovations.[14] Still, Maybie and Edmond were more concerned with the gaming potential of the venture. Perhaps more worrisome was the bad luck, which dogged the Moulin Rouge. More accurately, the historic place continued to have financial difficulties, but the Moulin Rouge was no different from any other hotel-casino business.

Maybie may always have been operating under the notion that wealthy investors might eventually buy the Moulin Rouge? Maybie realized the difficulty and ambiguity of his flagging hotel-casino business, and the tiresome relationship he was having with the black community. The strain of running and improving the operation may finally have gotten to him. In retrospect, however, it is worth noting that in the six years that Maybie owned the Moulin Rouge, he did make a significant contribution to the fabric of the black community by trying to keep the dream of the establishment going. But in the end, Maybie would be beaten, just like Sarann Knight-Preddy, who sadly lost her life savings operating the Moulin Rouge.[15]

Perhaps Bart Maybie began to realize the limitations of the place when on May 29, 2003, flames destroyed the landmark casino building, burning priceless memorabilia and photographs during a three-alarm fire.[16] Consequently, the venerable Moulin Rouge was brought down by a blazing fire. But the fire left the famous cursive neon marquee sign intact. According to journalist Jen Lawson, "Structural engineers determined that part of the front wall, the marquee, the vintage neon sign, three mosaic-tile covered columns and a tower that loom[ed] above the casino [could] be retained," after the fire.[17] It was later determined that arson was responsible for the fire, which happened five days after the 48th anniversary of the opening of the Moulin Rouge.[18]

The gutted Moulin Rouge after the May 29, 2003, fire (Earnest N. Bracey).

Maybie suspected arsonists, but he personally vowed to rebuild the burned-out place, proclaiming that the Moulin Rouge would rise again from the proverbial ashes, no matter what. Maybie predicted that the groundbreaking of a $200 million Moulin Rouge resort would start in 2005. It would be built in "three phases" ... with "a projected completion date for the first phase" in 2006, "with the other two phases completed by 2008."[19] But this ambitious renovation plan never occurred because Maybie would eventually strike a deal with the Moulin Rouge Development Corporation, a group of black businessmen and investors, to purchase the property for $12.1 million.[20]

The new black investors bought the historic hotel and casino — warts and all — despite the fire damage and multimillion-dollar price tag. Perhaps Maybie gave up on the Moulin Rouge because he could afford to, and because his CBC Financial Corporation would make an enormous profit. It was again a historic moment. The blunt reality was that Maybie might have done anything to get back almost all the money his corporation invested in the place to keep it afloat. But was it a losing proposition?

Chapter Nineteen

The New Black Entrepreneurs

The new black owners of the Moulin Rouge Development Corporation stood on the brink of a historical opportunity, although the principals, Chauncey Moore, Dale Scott and Rod Bickerstaff, initially had "a few glitches in financing,"[1] especially in terms of closing escrow. The Moulin Rouge lost money because of its location and from being mired continuously in controversy. Many in the Las Vegas community were stunned by the unexpected deal Bart Maybie made with the Moulin Rouge Development Corporation. Some black residents felt duped by Maybie's lack of commitment to the historic property, and the restoration.

Some believed that Maybie did a disservice to the black community. Many thought he had actually promised them a new place, a modern hotel-casino that blacks could consider their own. But perhaps a Moulin Rouge renaissance was never meant to be, as many watched warily as the legendary place finally succumbed to an arsonist's fire. In a sense, the place had "smoldered for decades," like an inactive volcano, even if it was, from time to time, fully operational. Indeed, as we have seen, the Moulin Rouge had been in disrepair and "lived a lie for nearly 50 years."[2] Indeed, before the massive, raging fire, because "there were no working sprinklers in the [main] building,"[3] the place was considered nothing more than "a shell of its former self— virtually a large snack shop with a bar."[4]

The ravaged Moulin Rouge has now been identified as a historically endangered place.[5] Therefore, when the new black owners took over, they again raised hope that the Moulin Rouge would be rehabilitated, or that the long-expected redevelopment project would be finally realized.[6] The new black owners had to have been painfully aware of the 50-year history of the burnt-out establishment. Indeed, the once-opulent hotel and casino, "suffered about $5 million in damage from the fire."[7] Why would *anyone* want to buy such an unprofitable, neglected place? Apparently, the black principals were confident enough to take on the project, but it is still a considerable challenge.

What probably mattered more was whether the new black owners of the Moulin Rouge would do *anything*, given the time and circumstances in Las Vegas. According to investor-principal Dale Scott in 2004, the black owners had to scale down plans for a $200 million renovation, which would have included "500 hotel rooms, 20 corporate suites and a 40,000-square-foot casino,"[8] in order to get the new Moulin Rouge built. These proposed plans were similar to what both Sarann Knight-Preddy and Bart Maybie wanted to accomplish, but as Scott succinctly explained, the historical place would have been built in short phases, "beginning with [a] $25 million first phase" that would have included "rebuilding the Moulin Rouge," from top to bottom, and "refurbishing the existing hotel."[9] Hence, the Moulin Rouge would not resemble its original incarnation.

The new black owners thought that purchasing the well-known place would further broaden their group's business portfolio, especially if they could get financing from Invest International Holdings, Pennsylvania lenders.[10] As of this writing, however, no deal has been completed. So it is unlikely that the controversial Moulin Rouge will be rebuilt anytime soon. Many in the black community empathized with the new black owners of the Moulin Rouge. Some even see them as visionaries, but many also know how apathetic city officials most likely will be, and how they may try to put unnecessary roadblocks in the way of the new black owners, in getting the historic place rebuilt.

Maybe the Moulin Rouge is just not far enough away from the Strip to be completely ignored? Some black residents continue to hope, but many are unsure whether *anyone* will ever come to a new or renovated Moulin Rouge. Some in the Las Vegas community even say that the plans for the place are inadequate. One observer, for example, recently stated that a hotel-casino on the same property just wouldn't work.[11] Such doubts are echoed by others. Indeed, as the same observer sarcastically puts it: "There aren't enough black gamblers in the community."[12] Although a lot has changed in Las Vegas since integration, especially in terms of race relations, many black Las Vegans feel they haven't found "their promised place at the American [economic] table...."[13] The problem is that matters of poverty and race haven't changed significantly in Las Vegas. The prosperity of the city has not been shared fully with the black population, even though a lot of strides have been made.

Clearly, for some in the city, the bad memories of segregation and racial discrimination haven't been erased, and they linger. Even today, as in the past, some blacks in Las Vegas have suffered greatly. Some indignities toward blacks still go on. Generally speaking, white Las Vegans feel that past racial and societal discrimination that they inflicted upon blacks in Las Vegas is water under the bridge. But curiously, this attitude on the part of whites in the city hasn't opened up new opportunities for all its black citizens. Is this because white Las Vegans fear blacks in general? According to journalist Jim Myers, "One of the biggest obstacles black Americans face is white fear of black people."[14] In a similar vein, Professor Charles W. Mills writes: "When some blacks progress upward into the middle class, then, their advance is actually a source of psychic discomfort for some whites. Those whites experience a malaise that is independent of objective downward mobility or stagnation measured by more conventional economic metrics; it inheres in the sense that things are going badly because (whether they are consciously aware of it or not) they are no longer so far removed from blacks."[15]

It is important to understand what Mills is saying, as well as how some whites in Las Vegas might feel about blacks and their quest for upward mobility in terms of owning lucrative businesses and casinos. Suffice it to say, the majority of the top casino executives in Las Vegas are white.[16] You can count the few exceptions on one hand. Most black gaming executives serve in human resources and diversity positions, but "former judge and Mississippi gaming regulator Lorenzo Creighton held several executive positions with Park Place Entertainment before becoming president of the Flamingo."[17] The only black person who owns a hotel-casino in Las Vegas, besides the owners of the Moulin Rouge, is Detroit construction and real estate millionaire Don Barden, who operates downtown's Fitzgeralds.[18]

In 2007, some wealthy black investors, and developer Donahue Peebles announced plans to build a $2.5 billion non-gaming resort on Paradise Road in the city, just east of the Wynn Las Vegas Golf Course.[19] This billion-dollar development, however, will not just cater to blacks. If this unnamed place is ever built or completed, "the 4.5 million square-foot project will be the largest real estate development in the country by an African American."[20]

But even with such positive changes, some black Las Vegans are no better off than they were during the 1950s. And with mostly white executives running the majority of hotel-casinos, the racial gap between the rich and poor in Las Vegas is still quite evident. Thus, with an increasingly growing population, all is still not well with Las Vegas. Blacks increasingly suspect that things will not change for them in the near future. Many recognize who the true power-brokers are, none of them black Americans.

The Moulin Rouge has largely gone unnoticed, but has not been ignored totally by the city fathers and gaming power brokers, or the city's rich and powerful residents. Many of those whites in power see the black owners of the Moulin Rouge as an abstraction, not real players in the gaming business in Las Vegas. Although the new black owners' ideas for building are not really hard to understand, there is still a lot of resistance by the city government. Perhaps the sheer magnitude of the project is too difficult for some of them to understand. Another potential problem, though, could be the rising costs for building. In any case, the new black owners are bullish on the potential of the Moulin Rouge, and their hard-driving acquisition of it shows their commitment to the black community, and the city of Las Vegas.

Still, many believe that there is too much uncertainty in rebuilding the Moulin Rouge, given its sad history. In some quarters, enthusiasm for building a new hotel-casino on the blighted property has been rejected. Naysayers don't believe the Moulin Rouge can become a viable player in the casino business in Las Vegas. Some think that renovating the place is misguided. Indeed, trying to rebuild the place on a hodgepodge basis just won't do. But the current black owners do not share the naysayers' suspicions.

Ultimately, they will decide what ideas for rebuilding the Moulin Rouge will be implemented. They believe that the historic place should be the center of the black community. A revitalized Moulin Rouge would help the depressed, rundown neighborhood. Simply renovating the Moulin Rouge, which is still listed on the national register of Historic Places,[21] is impossible, because much of it suffered severely from the fire on May 29, 2003. Indeed, the place has been reduced almost to rubble, razed to the ground. The main casino building has been almost totally obliterated. And things that once gave the Moulin Rouge its unique identity are gone. Historic preservationists, perhaps, winced painfully when they heard that the place had burned down.

But the main Desert Breeze apartments and some hotel rooms, which are considered a part of the Moulin Rouge complex, are still standing, but in much need of repair.[22] The Desert Breeze apartments were once used as low-income housing for poor residents. The new black owners have taken certain precautions to prevent any more damage to the place. Journalist Timothy Pratt writes that the black principals "have gone from promising Las Vegas officials that they would fix the place so that dozens of poor tenants can live decent lives to promising to find ... other places" for the tenants to live — that is, until the place is completely rebuilt.[23] All in all, the new black owners' optimism for restoring what is left or building a new place called the Moulin Rouge might seem quixotic, but they still believe it will happen, if everything goes as planned.

But as of this writing, the place is a poor example to the black community on the Westside. And until more tangible changes are made, or the hotel-casino is completed, visitors will only be able to gawk at the former greatness of the Moulin Rouge. The rebuilding is certainly not happening with any ferocity. The new black owners deserve credit for at least trying, even though they are outsiders, with no real ties to the black community in Las Vegas. But these black investors are sensitive to the black Westside neighborhood. Indeed, they are moving slowly, but surely, in their acquisitions. More importantly, some of their ideas about what they want to do to the property are unique. In the end, this might be a very good thing.

The new black owners firmly believe that rebuilding the Moulin Rouge must be accomplished on a significant scale, perhaps along the lines of the Palms Casino Hotel, a small resort located west of the Las Vegas Strip. The Palms Casino Hotel has been an enormous success story, and "a popular destination for many, especially with the younger crowd and Hollywood celebrities, despite the fact that it is located off the Strip."[24] Can the owners of the Moulin Rouge do a similar thing with the off–Strip property at 900 W. Bonanza Road? It remains to be seen. The new black owners speculate that a hotel-casino in a totally familiar location has a better-than-average chance of succeeding. But there are still those who believe that the Moulin Rouge will not work in today's cutthroat casino environment in its current, familiar location and presentation.

The historic place and its neighborhood are now almost universally shunned by whites, because of racism and perceived crimes. It is "not exactly the most desirable place to live."[25] But a new hotel-casino could draw the curious and history buffs. More importantly, how would a new, revitalized Moulin Rouge, which would probably dwarf the old structure, affect the more traditional homes and businesses in the surrounding area? Perhaps the area around the Moulin Rouge will have the same controversies in the future as in the past.

Some would prefer to see the Moulin Rouge demolished, if the rebuilding doesn't work out. Clearly, new buildings may be a long time in coming. Will the new black owners even get on the ball and actually fix the many problems at the Moulin Rouge? Indeed, does it make economic sense to rebuild? What will it take for the place to be in ideal condition today?

It seems the new black owners are not energetically trying to build. But they are not discouraged. No one really knows for certain what is happening behind the scenes at the Moulin Rouge, but the black owners think that the Moulin Rouge can eventually be in the same league as other successful resorts in Las Vegas, with an enormous, modern building, the likes of which the Westside has never seen. But the depressed property, unfortunately, suffers from almost intractable problems. A recent setback was the death of James Crook, a 67-year-old man, from pneumonia in January 2007 in one of the low-rent hotel rooms.[26]

According to journalist Timothy Pratt, "Crook's death was the outcome of a rock-and-a-hard-place scenario common to poor people seeking a place to live in the Las Vegas Valley."[27] In fairness, many of the evicted Moulin Rouge tenants refused to leave the hotel after being asked to vacate the premises. Prior to Crook's death, Stanton Wilkerson, an administrator at the historic place, stated that, "he issued 30-day eviction notices to about 70 of the hotel's 101 rooms"[28] in August 2006. Many went unheeded, even when the heat and hot water was eventually turned off. About this matter, Pratt wrote: "The situation at the [Moulin Rouge] hotel involved tenants living month to month and paying half the valley's average rent; county health officials discovering bedbugs, backed-up toilets and broken sinks; owners attempting to evict tenants to bring the hotel up to code; and tenants refusing to leave."[29]

It seems that hardly anyone in Las Vegas cares much about poor black people and the homeless. Is this because racial inequality still exist in the city, but in more subtle and persistent ways? Or is it that blacks, generally, are still at the economic bottom, even in the twenty-first century? The real question, ultimately, is why haven't some blacks been able to climb the steps of economic opportunity? Indeed, it seems no matter how hard black residents have tried to fit in and make things work in Las Vegas, they probably will never be really rich or prosper in the city. Is this because some social problems are also being ignored? Or will the rich and powerful in Las Vegas hinder such efforts? Blacks are not top casino executives or leaders of wealthy businesses on the Strip. Although some dispute that blacks in the city lack equality of opportunity, blacks should rise in greater numbers professionally in the casino business. In the final analysis, many blacks in the city don't believe that there is *anything* noble about Las Vegas.

Many of the poor blacks in Las Vegas today seem unaware of the historical importance of the Moulin Rouge — nor do they care. In fact, many don't spend a lot of time thinking about the place as being the first integrated hotel and casino. Therefore, keeping the place operating and in the mind of the black community and Las Vegas is becoming more of an issue every day. The black owners know that rebuilding the Moulin Rouge will be a hugely complex and difficult endeavor. If ever completed, however, it could be a prototype for new kinds of business developments that could be brought to the blighted Westside, perhaps triggering a rebirth of a vibrant black community.

Many have suggested that rebuilding the Moulin Rouge should start from scratch. What will provide the momentum to start the new Moulin Rouge? The black owners acknowledge that many people would appreciate a specific time frame. Moulin Rouge administrator Wilkerson has rightly and continuously pointed out that "the underlying goal ... has long been to reopen the Moulin Rouge's casino," which "is part of the

Another view of the Desert Breeze Apartments on West Bonanza, Las Vegas, Nevada, 2007 (Earnest N. Bracey).

massive overhaul planned ... of the sprawling Bonanza Road site, which includes the Moulin Rouge and the Desert Breeze, another 160 or so affordable apartments."[30]

Given the complexities of rebuilding the place, it would be fair to rely more on reason than on hope and prayer that things will one day get better at the Moulin Rouge. At some point, a financial commitment must be made for the revitalization efforts. Perhaps this is one of the biggest impediments to rebuilding. And constructing a new building is also subject to approval by the city government. Both of these factors have profound implications for the uncertain prospect of rebuilding. But at some point, a firm decision must be made about the revitalization of the Moulin Rouge. The final question is whether a new Moulin Rouge is what the city needs, and what people visiting Las Vegas actually want.

It will take a minor miracle for the Moulin Rouge to be revived to its former glory, no matter who owns it. Furthermore, keeping the Moulin Rouge afloat may be beyond the control of the new black owners right now. Meanwhile, they continue their hard work. The black principals believe that the Moulin Rouge will be rebuilt one day, and they are sure that nothing will prevent them from eventually realizing their dreams.

Not surprisingly, it is going to take some time to rebuild the historic place and get it back on track. It is hard to imagine something that isn't fully there yet. Such a place may never have the intimacy of the past Moulin Rouge. And it may never really represent the black community again, or have a significant impact on the city of Las Vegas. Ultimately, however, it might be up to members of the black community to voice their approval of a new Moulin Rouge, something for them to enjoy and to be proud of.

Chapter Twenty

Reflections on a Place and Time

This work is the first of its kind, a book of original scholarship on the history of the remarkable Moulin Rouge in Las Vegas. It moves from a historical narrative to concise political analysis, offering important and timely insights regarding the place and people, an unusual way of summing up a stunningly impressive hotel-casino property. It details the significance of the historic site, with a behind-the-scenes account of exactly what happened at the historic resort.

This treatment also debunks some mistaken ideas about the mysterious Moulin Rouge, clearing up disputed facts. For example, there was never a written agreement to end racial segregation in Las Vegas. But there was indeed a verbal agreement that took place at the Moulin Rouge between black and white leaders to fully integrate Las Vegas, the famous Strip, and the surrounding desert towns and cities. It was perhaps easy to imagine that racial desegregation was inevitable, not that things actually started out that way.

Whites in Las Vegas were determined to blunt the influence and political position of blacks in the city. And many blacks in the city felt desperate and hopeless, as well as psychologically crushed. In fact, blacks in the city were viewed as threatening and disruptive to the accepted social order, white rule, especially during the 1950s. It has been said that white privilege had for many years blinded white leaders in Las Vegas to the terrible injustices and social inequities imposed on the black population in the city.

Unfortunately, many Americans knew nothing about what was happening in Las Vegas during segregation until much later. But the racial discrimination occurring in the city came as no surprise to those who knew the unmitigated truth. Indeed, many more questions need to be asked about the tragic and racist past of Las Vegas. Gross discrimination against blacks was simply glossed over because white casino bosses didn't want to affect the booming and lucrative gaming industry and the gambling visitors coming to Las Vegas from throughout the nation and world.

This work also gives a thoroughly updated look at the circumstances of the Jim Crow era in Las Vegas, and the vital role the Moulin Rouge played in creating a truly cosmopolitan city. Furthermore, it describes the painful journey of blacks in Las Vegas, in the struggle for civil rights. Toward this end, this story shows the entire evolution of the Moulin Rouge, "the first multiracial or integrated or cosmopolitan hotel in Las Vegas,"[1] as it was considered "ground zero for the civil rights movement in Southern Nevada."[2] The Moulin Rouge essentially allowed the great city to break down its old, stifling, suffocating and unfair racial barriers.

The research in this book additionally captures the essence of what life was like for blacks residing in Las Vegas from the 1950s to the present day, and it reveals how some in the black population continue to struggle with the past. Consider, for instance, that the majority of blacks in Las Vegas still live predominantly in the poorest of neighborhoods. And it is still absolutely true that casino owners are not friendly to the black community and their needs, especially financial. They do not provide significant jobs.

The white power structure, in the past, tried to scrupulously avoid the black community, because of racial prejudice. Whites in power in Las Vegas wanted things to remain the same, and vigorously tried to enforce their discriminatory policies of white rule. Blacks and whites were certainly on the opposite sides of the social and economic spectrums in Las Vegas. To be sure, the righteous fight for integration and racial equality produced remarkable levels of objection from hateful white people in Las Vegas.

Of course, the white power structure was adept at dodging the difficult questions of race and discrimination. But whites who controlled the city could not sidestep race-relations problems. But instead of finding solutions, white politicians in Las Vegas continually stalled, arguing that integration should be done gradually. This was an approach that blacks in the city rejected outright.

That the powers-that-be wanted to quietly ignore the real history of the inhumane treatment of blacks in Las Vegas is understandable. Nonetheless, the fateful story of the Moulin Rouge should prompt strong reactions, because of the valuable contributions this simple hotel made to Las Vegas and our society as a whole. No apologies were ever made to the black population for how wrongly it was treated by the city and Nevada state governments.

The white power structure knew full well that things were not equal in Las Vegas for the black community, especially in meeting their specific needs and social desires, until after the 1960s. Blacks in the city were trapped by unfair and dishonest social conventions that forbid them from fully participating in politics and speaking their considerable minds. Thus, it was hard for blacks in Las Vegas to escape the overwhelming misery, poverty and deprivation they confronted almost on a daily basis. Opportunities for blacks were extremely limited.

White leaders in Las Vegas initially offered no answers, easy or otherwise, to the problems facing blacks, except to reject blacks' racial equality and their constitutional rights. Hence, it took courage to start the unlikely hotel-casino effort at the Moulin Rouge, to equalize things for black people, and end other insidious forms of racial segregation in the city. Indeed, creating the Moulin Rouge hotel and casino in 1955 on West Bonanza was hotly debated, but it was the culmination of a democratic idea. However, it was even thought at first, that building such a rogue establishment would be inconceivable, if not unsuccessful and impossible.

Objectively speaking, building the place tried to right a wrong, as it marked the beginning of the end of legal segregation in Las Vegas, and surrounding states and cities. Indeed, the opening of the Moulin Rouge coincided with the beginnings of the civil rights movement in the city. The legendary Moulin Rouge sparked "the civil-rights movement in Southern Nevada by ending segregation on the Strip."[3] Building the first integrated hotel-casino in the United States was calculated and necessary, because of the electric and poisonous atmosphere in Las Vegas during the 1950s and 1960s. Stark ideological differences between blacks and whites further deepened the racial divide in Las Vegas.

Many understood the political and social implications of operating such a controversial hotel and casino, because before such integrated places as the Moulin Rouge, throughout the United States "recreational activities, facilities, and support for blacks were universally inadequate."[4] Blacks in fact had no illusion about their limits in a racist society, especially if they wanted to travel or go on vacation.

Entrenched segregation was characteristic of most white businesses where blacks sought entertainment and recreation. According to Professor Jearold Winston Holland, blacks during the 1950s and 1960s who dared to travel "outside their immediate communities, especially in the South [or to places like Las Vegas] had to make arrangements to stay in private homes or black schools because white hotels would not accommodate them."[5] Even so, the Moulin Rouge was built by mostly white businessmen, in full knowledge that it would stir up racial troubles. They did not care about the racial problems of the day, because building hotels and casinos was all about making fast money, all the time.

In a growing city like Las Vegas, dominated by privileged whites and some disreputable people, segregation was perhaps an embarrassment to those who sympathized with the plight of poor blacks. Journalist and author Steve Fischer put it this way:

> It was the middle of the 20th century, and most of the black entertainers in Las Vegas in the 1940s and early 1950s went to West Las Vegas to sleep and eat. West Las Vegas at that time was pretty bad. Muddy streets. Little plumbing, little electricity. That's where most of the black entertainers who worked in Las Vegas lived, as did the maids and the kitchen help. Even Sammy Davis, Jr., and his dad, Sammy Davis, Sr., and his uncle Will Mastin, stayed in the rooming houses in that poor section of town; there were laws back then about such things.[6]

In so many words, black Las Vegans had to endure numerous humiliations because of the racism of that day, especially in regards to recreational accommodations. And "this discrimination in lodging and eating would have lasting effects on blacks and their recreation and leisure."[7] Holland goes on to write that "since travel itself is often viewed as a form of recreation and as a means of access to other leisure pursuits [like gambling in Las Vegas], black opportunity was very much affected by segregation."[8]

But after the Moulin Rouge was built with much protest and fanfare, it had an uncertain future, even with its early success. At first it was "assumed that the Moulin Rouge was going to attract blacks only," but later white gamblers came out in droves to the popular hotel-casino, much to the chagrin and surprise of almost everyone.[9] Therefore, white casino bosses did almost *everything* to undermine the new place — from threats of violence to individuals that supported the place, to outright sabotage by cutting off food and liquor supplies.

To fully understand, blacks in Las Vegas at one time were not seen as human beings with fundamental rights, which reflected a maddening hypocrisy of those whites who talked about equal justice and the rule of law. Further, black Las Vegans knew that the many promises made by the government to address racial injustices were mostly empty. Moreover, "during the Jim Crow years there was a definite caste system under which blacks were expected to conduct themselves as the lowest caste."[10] But blacks refused to accept their destiny as the lowest of the low.

What started as political protest in the city quickly turned into a protracted battle, a continuous civil rights movement. Black Las Vegans' displeasure grew more vocal and demanding, while whites were afraid of desegregation like most of the nation. The voice of the black community in Las Vegas fell on deaf ears, which inflamed the feelings of racial hatred in the state of Nevada, not just in the segregated South during the 1950s. In point of fact, blacks in Las Vegas vigorously rebelled.

Many blacks in Las Vegas warned the white citizens in the city that stopping the civil rights movement was fruitless. It was not until the propitious meeting at the Moulin Rouge hotel and casino in 1960 that white city leaders, who lacked a coherent notion of what they should do, finally got involved in changing the Jim Crow racism that existed in the city. The powerful racial tensions in Las Vegas could not be ignored, but it was understandable that some black people could not have cared less about white citizens, as there was a long history of justice denied to blacks in Las Vegas. Poverty, unemployment and disillusionment were the order of the day for most blacks during 1950s and 1960s.

Nevertheless, black and white leaders feverishly worked to end racial discrimination in the city. Some blacks in Las Vegas, as we have seen, were quickly disillusioned by the nonviolence of the early civil rights movement. For some radical blacks, violence was the only answer. Radical black Las Vegans believed that the white power structure should be eliminated to effect a truly heterogeneous and equal society. Many of these radical blacks in Las Vegas, no doubt, ignited fears of racial violence. In truth, according to Holland, "Those who feel society treats them as inferior may react in ways that appear defensive and aggressive, even in disruptive and potentially anti-social behavior."[11] But there was always the question of societal discrimination in Las Vegas, as the black population tried to adhere to nonviolence to achieve its goal of racial equality.

It was against this racial segregation context that the Moulin Rouge was possible. It was critical to discuss the future of race relations at a time when this was considered irrelevant, and even though there was a difference of opinions on what path blacks and whites should take in Las Vegas. Surprisingly, the Moulin Rouge evolved, expanded and changed over a period of years with mixed success. It was a colossal failure later and in its first iteration — that is, compared with the mega-casino resorts that were slowly being built on the Strip — and even though "the Moulin Rouge was making money."[12]

Sadly, its first existence was short-lived. Still, the invincible Moulin Rouge gave many downtrodden black people an opportunity to do something exciting and meaningful inside the Las Vegas community, as well as for themselves. According to professors Ollie A. Johnson III and Karin L. Stanford, black American organizations "are generally structured in ways that give high-ranking officials substantial authority and influence,"[13] especially in the day-to-day operations of a business like a Las Vegas hotel-casino. But the Moulin Rouge was not originally a black business.

In terms of the staff, for example, from the onset, according to Fischer, "all the dealers at the Rouge were white."[14] Fischer goes on to note that before the Moulin Rouge was established, most blacks in Las Vegas "couldn't deal or be involved in any casino games."[15]

Fischer explains that "there were no experienced dealers to draw from."[16] But this was patently untrue. To the contrary, you only had to look as far as the many gaming and licensed all-black clubs and nightspots on the Westside to find some talented black dealers. Some might say that this slight was a blatant violation of the black community's rights, and a setback to their ongoing fight for higher paying hotel-casino jobs.

Be that as it may, even the Moulin Rouge would eventually have black ownership, and blacks successfully filling every position at the place. "Given the country's history of race relations and black minority status," the Moulin Rouge was a minor miracle that positively affected the entire black community. Indeed, "developments [inside] and outside the black community have always had major consequences for [black] Americans."[17] The beginning efforts were certainly profound.

Everyone wanted to see the great shows at the Moulin Rouge when the curtains came up at night. All in all, the development of the first integrated casino hotel in Las Vegas was a well thought-out initiative. Today, the Moulin Rouge is a very different place, because of years of neglect. But many in the black community would like once again to embrace the initial excitement of the Moulin Rouge during the 1950s.

The story of the Moulin Rouge is a remarkable tale, an ongoing episode in the life of Las Vegas, which must never be ignored. It seems almost everyone from that time-honored era of the 1950s has an amazing story to tell about what happened at the place, and somehow these stories must be recorded. For the Moulin Rouge to have existed at all was one of those great, unexplained "mysteries of history"[18] in Las Vegas, an example of frequently unknown places that really matter in the city.

Conclusion

The history of the Moulin Rouge is a synthesis of many sad stories of the black residents in the city of Las Vegas. But it is a remarkable and complicated story all the same. It should also serve as a reminder of the city's Jim Crow past. It was also not so long ago, during "the Rat Pack era, that gaming was the main draw and locals were a part of the [absolute] equation" in the city.[1] As many already know, the historic Moulin Rouge was once the hub of entertainment and gambling in the city of Las Vegas for black tourists, entertainers, and the black community, and it should be commended for that. The grand opening was a unique and fabulous experience for many in the city — both blacks and whites — as the Moulin Rouge once put on extravagant, theatrical shows that remained with you, perhaps, for as long as it took to watch. Everything seemed fine when the place first opened, but as we have seen, that did not last.

The chemistry of the Moulin Rouge during its glory days probably can never be duplicated, as it provided the kind of atmosphere that helped the rich and famous individuals of all stripes as well as the curious come together, meet, play, and mingle. Perhaps this was what made the Moulin Rouge so special and unique. Indeed, the place became a bold, race-relations experiment that ultimately unfolded in the desegregation of Las Vegas. It was also the first integrated hotel and casino — a fitting place, a reminder of the city's fragmented, tumultuous, racist past. Why did the white builders and investors undertake this specific project of historical significance? Probably because the time had arrived.

Despite its historical significance, the Moulin Rouge today is largely overlooked by visitors to the city. Right now, the rundown place doesn't get much attention from the local Las Vegas population, either. Many tourists and mega-high-rollers have a tendency to bypass the Westside, staying clear of the Moulin Rouge because of its adverse location, and the fact that it was literally destroyed by a catastrophic fire. The current look of the Moulin Rouge is that of a place ravaged by time on the sad fringes of Las Vegas. Despite all its former charm and individuality, the place is certainly an egregious eyesore today. But for a while the historic place put its wonderful stamp on the city.

The Moulin Rouge now looks like an abandoned, burnt-out building site, like a bombed-out shelter gone to seed in times of war, perhaps, instead of a sparkling new casino of the Bugsy Siegel era. Nowadays, the most impressive thing about the place is its still-standing tower and curvy marquee sign that reminds one of the skeletal remains of an eviscerated dinosaur, or prehistoric beast. Indeed, the metal scaffolding that now surrounds the Moulin Rouge and holds up the famous neon sign is an embarrassment to its former self, hardly a throwback to another, exciting time. For some, the Moulin Rouge is still a work in progress, but not a hotel-casino like the mega properties on the Strip today. But you cannot study the complete history of Las Vegas without discussing the erstwhile Moulin Rouge hotel and casino.

Furthermore, there is more to the Moulin Rouge story than meets the historical eye. As discussed in this work, it was truly astonishing that the place was even built. Having said this, the Moulin Rouge is perhaps the number one endangered historical landmark in Las Vegas, that is, if it is not rebuilt immediately. After all, the Moulin Rouge has always been unlike any other hotel-casino in Las Vegas because of its role in the black civil rights movement and racial integration efforts. In a nondescript meeting room at the place, black and white community leaders decided to totally desegregate Las Vegas.

Discriminatory practices made life extremely hard for blacks in Las Vegas. There was a tendency for whites to turn a blind eye to racial parochialism. Black entertainers were poorly treated, which was more disturbing than anything else. The Moulin Rouge provided solidarity in the black community, as the place gave blacks in Las Vegas a focal point while courageous black activists challenged the dominance of segregation. Blacks even found a way eventually to play a significant role in the politics of the city, when they encountered resistance when looking for work and casino jobs on the Strip.

Clearly, black activism was beneficial to black residents in the desert oasis of Las Vegas, especially in fighting Jim Crow racism and the discriminatory policies of the city government. Today, a more covert, perverse, and obscure racism exists in Las Vegas. The black middle-class in Las Vegas has remained static since the early 1980s. We must ask why this is so. Indeed, what must happen to empower the black community in Las Vegas today? This is important to understand because some black Las Vegans continue to be subjected to certain subtle forms of discrimination, especially in securing high-wage jobs on the glitzy Strip.

In the past, critics differed markedly about what should be done to level the playing field for blacks in Las Vegas. Perhaps, local officials were afraid of black people in some way during the 1950s, 1960s, and 1970s, especially when they finally recognized what city government collectively did or didn't do for the black population. Such hard questions have gone mostly unanswered today. Las Vegas is no longer the small, simple place it might have been in the past, with mega hotel-casinos now being built at a phenomenal rate. In a "me-too construction boom" in Las Vegas, casino owners say that this "growth is simply due to a host of innovations that make gambling more fun" and especially "more convenient."[2]

There was a time when old-fashioned codes of honor meant something in Las Vegas. But perhaps not today. So can the Moulin Rouge today use its marvelous and controversial history to spark the rebirth of the Westside, since Las Vegas has been aptly described as the city of reinvention?[3] The redevelopment of the Moulin Rouge could be good for the city of Las Vegas, and certainly a boom for the black neighborhood. Rebuilding the historic place might blunt the effect of the Westside area's economic slump, which began with desegregation in the 1960s.

But how can the Moulin Rouge be revitalized in a time of mega casinos like the ones built on the Strip? Indeed, what amount of local activism is necessary to start the building process at the Moulin Rouge? The predominantly black Westside has always been dogged by poverty, a sense of hopelessness, and a lack of high-wage jobs and new black businesses. Who should give to build the place back up? The area has had to deal with rigid building codes imposed by the City of Las Vegas, which may stand in the way of building a several-storied new structure. According to business writer Kim Clark, "brick-and-mortar casinos" are highly regulated.[4] But a new Moulin Rouge could indeed change the entire Westside area, prompting another renaissance through a new kind of urban development.

Indeed, a new Moulin Rouge could very well make a difference to the entire black community, as it might generate significant income for black businesses in the neighborhood. Rebuilding might also add a sort of connectiveness to the past, while allowing for accessibility and needed jobs. Perhaps revitalization of the Moulin Rouge could also contribute significantly to the stability of the Westside neighborhood, while building connections and networks across economic and racial lines, broadening opportunities to the local black residents. As president and chief executive officer of the Moulin Rouge Development Corporation, Dale Scott has firmly stated that rebuilding the historic site "would become the catalyst for redevelopment of the low-income neighborhood, which sits just north of downtown Las Vegas."[5]

Preserving the historic Moulin Rouge site will definitely provide a rare opportunity for the new black owners, as it could dominate the social fabric on the Westside in Las Vegas, and go a long way toward repairing the ailing black community. A live entertainment area would also be a boost to the residents of the Westside. The Moulin Rouge potentially could be a premiere destination for upwardly mobile tourists, given its historical importance, especially for those who want to learn about the city of Las Vegas. But that day may still be a long way away, given the tragic history and circumstances of the place. It is quite possible, however, that a whole new generation can learn about the infamous hotel and casino. And the niche possibilities for a new Moulin Rouge are endless.

Nonetheless, a revitalized Moulin Rouge might also have a negative effect on the local black residents, because some might worry about increased crime and traffic congestion in the area. A parking garage could remedy such traffic congestion concerns, however. Indeed, such concerns were similarly expressed over the building of the Palms Casino on the opposite off-Strip end of town. And the Palms Casino has been an overwhelming success. There have also been concerns about encroachment and urban sprawl, and how a new Moulin Rouge would affect nearby casinos, especially on the Strip and in downtown Las Vegas. There are further worries about whether the new black owners can maintain the operation in the low-income community. Maybe a new place would actually enhance the quality of life for the poor black residents of the area.

The idea of a new Moulin Rouge on the edge of the city may not appeal to the white power structure, as it may put a major crimp in the plan to build up the downtown Las Vegas area. In any case, some critics believe that a new Moulin Rouge is not going to work, not only because of its controversial location, but because of its racial history. Some also believe that rebuilding just isn't right considering the cultural circumstances. But a new establishment could also evolve in a different, positive way within the Las Vegas black community. More diversity and social interaction is still needed in the City of Lights. The revitalization of the Moulin Rouge would definitely have enough impact to transform the lives of many blacks on the Westside, while providing a significant economic windfall for minority businesses. Therefore, the city should realize that a new Moulin Rouge is not a threat to the Strip and downtown developments, because of the phenomenal growth of the city.

Nevertheless, some cynics are doubtful that a new and improved iteration of the Moulin Rouge will give blacks living in the area a voice in building and upgrading the surrounding neighborhood. In the final analysis, the degree to which the place can be rebuilt and attract patrons, as well as generate income, will determine the success or failure of a revitalized Moulin Rouge. Finally, the historic place could also cater to the fast-growing Latino community. Viewed superficially, many might say that reviving the Moulin Rouge is not that important. But what's at stake is not just the historical importance of the prestigious site, but whether the neighborhood will literally rise again in terms of providing business and revenue opportunities for the black community of Las Vegas.

Conclusion

Although the Moulin Rouge is certainly not what it used to be, the whole idea of renewing the historic site shouldn't be derailed in any way. But in its current, sad configuration, is the Moulin Rouge worthy of saving? Indeed, the place should not be maintained in its current condition without immediate improvements. Why haven't the new black owners moved to quickly bulldoze the old remnants of the place, making room for a new hotel-casino right away? Building a beautiful new hotel-casino is the key. It should fit in nicely with the rest of Las Vegas's mega-buildings. It seems hard to believe that the Moulin Rouge will ever be rebuilt, however, because of the cost. But a new hotel-casino in the black neighborhood will revive the poor area.

Indeed, rebuilding the Moulin Rouge is perhaps the most anticipated development on the Westside, as many see it as a means of renewal and hope for the black residents. The rebuilding will take the commitment of the entire Las Vegas community. A serious project like rebuilding the Moulin Rouge cannot be done in isolation. The city government and the people of the neighborhood must play a significant role. Indeed, fervent community support is sorely needed. But the truth is, it may never happen. Although the Moulin Rouge Development Corporation purchased 2.3 acres near the historic site at 920 West Bonanza Road for $4.3 million in March 2006[6] for further redevelopment, it may not be enough to save the celebrated Moulin Rouge.

The pressure ostensibly is on. But it remains to be seen if the history of the Moulin Rouge can repeat itself. The sincere effort to make the hotel-casino first rate is something we should take away from this discussion. On the other hand, there is the unmistakable suspicion that the place will never be resuscitated. When it is all said and done, the key to the redevelopment and restoration of the Moulin Rouge and the surrounding area lies with the new black owners and their ultimate goals. It definitely will be a preservation challenge. As of this writing, work is still being done to rebuild the place. But the site has a long way to go.

Perhaps the community will long remember the Moulin Rouge as a shining light of integration and diversity among hotels and casinos. But no matter what we might think about the remarkable place, some long-time residents believe that the Moulin Rouge is a national treasure, an irreplaceable historical landmark. Perhaps its future, if it is ever rebuilt, will be more about ambience and attitude than its past as the first integrated hotel-casino in Las Vegas. Mostly, the Moulin Rouge is a wonderful memorial, a testament to important things long past. There is hope that some type of building, probably modeled on the Las Vegas of yesteryear, with an evocative design, will be built on the Moulin Rouge site, which might be transformed into again an awe-inspiring, spectacular place. Indeed, a reinvented Moulin Rouge will always exist in the continuum of Las Vegas history. More broadly, let us hope that the famous Moulin Rouge hotel and casino and the surrounding area does not ultimately become a parking garage, or just another strip of asphalt in Las Vegas.

Postscript

After the first draft of this full history of the Moulin Rouge was completed, the black owners announced on October 5, 2007, that the remaining dilapidated buildings at the 900 West Bonanza site would be demolished, "within 60 days."[1] This revelation was good news, as it will be the next major evolution at the famous place. The Moulin Rouge and its contribution to the racial history and harmony of Las Vegas cannot be overstated. Indeed, as we have discussed, the "agreement between civic leaders and representatives of the National Association for the Advancement of Colored People that ended segregation" in the city was made at the interracial Moulin Rouge hotel and casino.[2]

The current effort to tear down the vacant 1950s buildings on the sad, 52-year-old property is only one piece of a larger puzzle — to build a new hotel-casino. Journalist Benjamin Spillman tells us that it would "mark the reversal of a run of unstable ownership, bankruptcy, deterioration, and vacancy that's plagued the former Moulin Rouge site for more than 50 years."[3] It appears that a reshaping, redesign, or redefinition of the first integrated hotel-casino is imminent. A rehabilitation of the historic site will come sooner now, it seems, than later.

The new black owners of the Moulin Rouge and their dreams of reviving the property will be finally realized. Without a doubt, such a re-imagination of the Moulin Rouge will be a hard challenge. It will certainly be a highly innovative undertaking. Press accounts indicate that a $300 million initial phase might break ground by mid–2009, "with completion in late 2010." The last phase would bring the property's size to 2 million square feet.[4] Apparently the black owners believe that their problems are surmountable. Nor are they embarrassed that the project has taken such a frustratingly long time. Matters at the place have never been easy.

The black owners may have experienced financial stress after acquiring the 15-acre site, but now it's been reported that they have the necessary financial backing from a source "outside Las Vegas" to complete the project.[5] The black owners have barely scratched the surface in reshaping a new Moulin Rouge, but now they envision "a 750-room hotel, more than 100,000 square feet of gaming and upscale amenities" that might possibly "attract local[s] and tourist traffic."[6] A new Moulin Rouge would provide a catalyzing business effect, as already mentioned, which would be tremendously important to black people in the city of Las Vegas.

While the black owners believe that things at the historic site are on solid ground, and that they are progressing in the right direction, some might say that the Moulin Rouge is still in sad state. Indeed, some see the restoration of the Moulin Rouge as a dicey proposition, and the location of the hotel-casino as a liability. Spillman, for example, writes that "the site's distance from other downtown casinos and the overall condition of the neighborhood work against any revival of the property."[7] The new black owners, however, are determined to revive the Moulin Rouge project, even in light of recent lawsuits.

There is no denying the spirit of the black owners as they continue to get their act together. They have now completed realistic plans for a totally new and improved hotel-casino resort, "incorporating the original structure's most recognizable features"[8] at the controversial location, such as the looming, trademark tower, paying reverence to a sterling, yesteryear past. Eventually they will submit firmer plans to the Las Vegas Planning Commission for approval.[9] Any speculation about not building on the expansive property because it is in a depressed area is preposterous. Many believe that the Moulin Rouge, historically "plagued with false starts and setbacks," is due for a long-planned makeover, given its "several failed rebirths."[10]

It is likely that the black owners feel an obligation to complete the endeavor no matter what, as they see the Moulin Rouge, "shuttered for decades," as the future of the surrounding neighborhood, despite the lack of any major black businesses or tourist attractions. Indeed, there is no doubt that the new black owners would like to put the tragic past of the intrepid Moulin Rouge behind them, and move forward, if possible. According to journalist Tony Illia: "A rebirth would bring 1950s Hollywood glamour together with Motown glitz in a Retro-modern package. Visitors, for instance, could create customized play lists online for their room before their arrival."[11]

In the end, will the new owners be able to turn around the fortunes of the Moulin Rouge? We may know something soon about the actual rebuilding of the Moulin Rouge — or perhaps we might be kept guessing.

Chapter Notes

Preface

1. Gary Dretzka, "Gambling on Tradition," *Chicago Tribune* (February 6, 1996), p. 3. See also Christel Wheeler, "Don't Look Back: History, Which Never Was a Big Money-Maker Anyway, Faces the Wrecking Ball," *Las Vegas City Life* (August 29, 1996), p. 13–14.

2. M.L. Miranda, *A History of Hispanics in Southern Nevada* (Reno, Nevada: University of Nevada Press, 1997), p. 147.

3. Geoff Schumacher, *Sun, Sin & Suburbia: An Essential History of Modern Las Vegas* (Las Vegas, Nevada: Stephen Press, 2004), p. 42.

Introduction

1. Kenneth Minogue, *Politics* (New York: Oxford University Press, 1995), p. 108.

2. Katherine Best and Katherine Hillyer, *Las Vegas: Play Town U.S.A.* (New York: David McKay, 1955), p. 139.

3. Elmer Rusco, "Letter to the Editor," *Nevada Historical Society Quarterly* (September 21, 1991), p. 1. Original copy of letter in author's possession.

4. *Ibid.*

5. *Ibid.* Sadly, it was the unjust policies of the state that created racial segregation in the first place in Nevada, despite what has been written to the contrary.

6. Erik C. Huey, "Fitzgeralds owner upbeat on downtown," *Las Vegas Review-Journal* (February 20, 2004), p. 2D. Many of the past discrimination problems were blamed on black Las Vegans themselves, which was indeed outrageous.

7. Ed Koch, "Blaze is latest chapter in hotel's storied history," *Las Vegas Sun* (May 29, 2003), p. 9A.

8. Eugene P. Moehring and Michael S. Green, *Las Vegas: A Centennial History* (Reno and Las Vegas: University of Nevada Press, 2005), p. 215.

9. Michael Squires, "Group buys historic site," *Las Vegas Review-Journal* (January 29, 2004), p. 1B. We should marvel at the complexity and size of the proposed new Moulin Rouge project. Perhaps the idea of rebuilding the place isn't as far-fetched as one might imagine.

10. *Ibid.*, p. 6B. The black owners never believed that they were plunging into

something blindly by purchasing the Moulin Rouge. But the important project will require all of their effort and sacrifice.

11. *Ibid.* Another off-the-Strip property, the Red Rock Resort on West Charleston Boulevard, has become a successful hotel-casino and "a popular destination for many who live near it." See Joe Schoenmann, "Tower plan met with 'oohs,' casino with 'ews,'" *Las Vegas Sun* (September 23, 2007), p. 9.

12. *Ibid.*

Chapter One

1. "Moulin Rouge Hotel," *Wikipedia, the free encyclopedia,* http://en.wikipedia.org/wiki/Moulin_Rouge_Hotel, p. 1.

2. Haya El Nasser, "Las Vegas moving from a circus act to a regular city," *USA Today* (February 28, 2006), p. 1A.

3. "Hotel History: Moulin Rouge Hotel & Casino," *Las Vegas Now* (Las Vegas Centennial, 2005), p. 71.

4. Leon F. Litwack, *Trouble in Mind: Black Southerners in the Age of Jim Crow* (New York: Alfred A. Knopf, 1998), p. 229.

5. "Hotel History: Moulin Rouge Hotel & Casino." According to Professor William J. Wilson, racism in the public school system was more subtle and indirect. See William J. Wilson, "The Significance of Social and Racial Prisms," in *Through Different Eyes: Black and White Perspectives on American Race Relations,* edited by Peter Rose, Stanley Rothman, and William J. Wilson (New York: Oxford University Press, 1973), p. 407.

6. Earnest N. Bracey, "The Moulin Rouge Mystique: Blacks and Equal Rights in Las Vegas," *Nevada Historical Society Quarterly,* Vol. 39, No. 4 (Winter 1996), p. 272.

7. "We Shall Overcome — Moulin Rouge," http://www.cr.nps.gov/nr/travel/civil rights/nv1.htm, 12/16/2006, p. 1. Whites living in the general location underwent much angst at the building of the Moulin Rouge. According to historian Eugene P. Moehring, when the Moulin Rouge "was being considered by city commissioners in March 1954, Bonanza-area residents, who were mostly white, vehemently opposed its construction." See Eugene P. Moehring, *Resort City in the Sunbelt, Las Vegas, 1930–2000* (Reno and Las Vegas: University of Nevada Press, 2000), p. 183.

8. Litwack, *Trouble in Mind,* p. 231.

9. Eugene P. Moehring. *Resort City in the Sunbelt,* p. 182.

10. William J. Wilson, "The Significance of Social and Racial Prisms," *Through Different Eyes: Black and White Perspectives on American Race Relations,* edited by Peter I. Rose, Stanley Rothman, and William J. Wilson (New York: Oxford University Press, 1973), p. 207.

11. *Ibid.,* p. 397.

12. *Ibid.,* pp. 396–397.

13. Katharine Best and Katharine Hillyer. *Las Vegas: Playtown U.S.A.* (New York: David McKay, 1955), p. 136.

14. Annelise Orleck. *Storming Caesars Palace: How Black Mothers Fought Their Own War on Poverty* (Boston, Mass.: Beacon Press, 2005), p. 63.

15. Moehring, *Resort City in the Sunbelt*, p. 182.

16. Orleck, *Storming Caesars Palace*, p. 62.

17. Earnest N. Bracey, "Migration of Blacks to Las Vegas, Nevada," *Encyclopedia of the Great Black Migration*, Volume 1: A-L, edited by Steven A. Reich (Westport, Conn.: Greenwood Press, 2006), p. 486.

18. *Ibid.*

19. Moehring, *Resort City*, p. 182.

20. *Ibid.*

21. Trish Geran, *Beyond the Glimmering Light: The Pride and Perseverance of African Americans in Las Vegas* (Las Vegas: Stephens Press, 2006), p. 121.

22. Bracey, "The Moulin Rouge Mystique," p. 274.

23. *Ibid.*

24. Geran, *Beyond the Glimmering Light*, p. 120. Note that Joe Louis later became an official host at Caesars Palace, when the Strip was finally integrated.

25. Bracey, "The Moulin Rouge Mystique," p. 272.

Chapter Two

1. Benjamin Spillman, "Moulin Rouge taps Epic Gaming," *Las Vegas Review-Journal* (March 6, 2008), p. 3D.

2. Matt Keleman, "Hidden Histories," *City Life* (December 9–15, 2004), p. 18 (pp. 16–19).

3. Spillman, "Moulin Rouge taps Epic Gaming," p. 3D.

4. Keleman, "Hidden Histories," p. 17. Dr. Bob Bailey was later able to investigate discrimination in the areas of employment and education when he became, in 1961, the chairman of Nevada's Equal Rights Commission. Bailey also became the emcee of the Moulin Rouge when it first opened.

5. *Ibid.*, p. 18. Additionally, blacks "were systematically evicted from Downtown, and directed across the railroad tracks to the derelict streets of West Las Vegas," especially when black Las Vegans tried to buy land or open businesses on the Strip. See Nefretti Makenta, "A View from West Las Vegas," in David Littlejohn, editor, *The Real Las Vegas: Life Beyond the Strip* (New York: Oxford University Press, 1999), p. 110.

6. James Goodrich, "Negroes Can't Win in Las Vegas," *Ebony*, Vol. 1 (1954), p. 45.

7. Robert A. Goldwin, "The U.S. Constitution Guarantees Social Justice," in Carol Wekesser and Karin Swisher, editors, *Social Justice: Opposing Viewpoints* (San Diego, Calif.: Greenhaven Press, 1990), p. 24.

8. Keleman, "Hidden Histories," p. 18.

9. Earnest N. Bracey, "The Migration of Blacks to Las Vegas," in Steven A. Reich, editor, *Encyclopedia of the Great Black Migration*, Volume 1: A-L (Westport, Conn.: Greenwood Press, 2006), p. 485. Perhaps at one time in Las Vegas, all blacks knew each other because of the small size of the black population, and perhaps this made the various linkages possible, especially in the fight against discriminatory policies by the white community and local government.

10. Keleman, "Hidden Histories," p. 18. According to the late University of Nevada professor, Elmer R. Rusco, "It [seemed] highly likely that the high concen-

tration of blacks in West Las Vegas, as well as the malapportionment of the Legislature, and the interaction of partisanship with malapportionment [perhaps helped] to explain why Nevada [and Las Vegas] came so late to the civil rights fold." Some black scholars, however, would disagree with the simplicity of Rusco's argument, calling it another excuse for persistent discrimination against blacks in Las Vegas. See Elmer R. Rusco, "The Civil Rights Movement in Nevada," *Nevada Public Affairs Review* (1987), p. 81.

11. *Ibid.*

12. Roosevelt Fitzgerald, "Black Entertainers in Las Vegas: 1940–1960." Unpublished paper in author's possession, p. 19.

13. John M. Findlay. *People of Chance: Gambling in American Society from Jamestown to Las Vegas* (New York: Oxford University Press, 1986), p. 189.

14. Shaun McKinnon, "Boundaries of Race Tumble," *Las Vegas Review-Journal* (April 26, 1993), pp. 1A and 4A.

15. Keleman, "Hidden Histories," p. 18.

16. Larry Werner, "Black Pride: Rich Culture, History, Legacy of Southern Nevada Black Community," *Las Vegas Review-Journal* (February 7, 1983), P. 2B.

Chapter Three

1. Gary E. Elliott, "The Moulin Rouge Hotel: A Critical Appraisal of a Las Vegas Legend," unpublished paper, p. 1.

2. Geran, *Beyond the Glimmering Light,* p. 121.

3. Elliott, "The Moulin Rouge Hotel," p. 6.

4. Kristi Goodwin, "Putting a New Face on the Past," *Las Vegas Style* (November 1992), p. 16.

5. Tom Flagg, "The Joint Jumped All Night: The Moulin Rouge: Harbinger of Integration in Las Vegas," *Oasis: The Magazine of the University of Nevada, Las Vegas* (Autumn 1991), p. 9. See also Bracey, "Moulin Rouge Mystique," p. 272.

6. Mary M. Gafford, "Las Vegas' First Integrated Casino," *Las Vegas Centennial 1905–2005: Tell Your Best Vegas Story*, (posted Sept. 21, 2005), http://www.lasvegas2005.org/interactive/lvstory77.html, p. 1.

7. "We Shall Overcome — Moulin Rouge," http://www.cr.nps.gov/nr/travel/civilrights/ nv1.htm, 12/16/2006, p. 1.

8. *Ibid.*

9. Goodwin, "Putting a New Face on the Past," p. 16.

10. *Ibid.*

11. Claytee D. White, "African American History in the West Vignette: The Moulin Rouge," *Vignette: The Moulin Rouge*, http://faculty.washington.edu/9taylor/aa_vignettes/org_moulin_rouge, 12/16/2006, p. 1.

12. *Ibid.* According to the collection edition of the Moulin Rouge 38th Year Birthday Celebration brochure, "No expense had been spared to make the hotel a lavish showplace. The owners-operators contracted with the late Pat Patterson, California's famed black maitre d,' who, in advance of the opening, had scoured the country recruiting waiters and waitresses to provide the meticulous service that Patterson demanded of those who worked under his supervision." (May 21–23, 1993), p. 2. For-

mer black owner Sarann Knight-Preddy also recalled that the food was excellent because some of the cooks were brought from Paris, France. See Jerry Fink, "Not Forgotten," *Las Vegas Sun* (October 22, 2000), p. 6E.

13. *Ibid.* See also "Moulin Rouge: A Stroll Down Memory Lane," videocassette, with emcee Bob Bailey. Moulin Rouge Hotel & Casino, Las Vegas, Nevada, October 30, 1992.

14. *Ibid.*

15. Orleck, *Storming Caesars Palace,* pp. 64–65.

16. Flagg, "The Joint Jumped All Night: The Moulin Rouge: Harbinger of Integration in Las Vegas," p. 10.

17. *Ibid.*

18. Bracey, "The Moulin Rouge Mystique," pp. 279–280.

19. *Ibid.*, p. 280.

20. Larry Werner, "Black Pride: Rich culture, history, legacy of Southern Nevada black community," *Las Vegas Review-Journal* (February 7, 1983), p. 1B.

21. Goodwin, "Putting a New Face," p. 16.

22. Werner, "Black Pride," p. 1B.

23. "We Shall Overcome — Moulin Rouge Hotel," p. 1.

24. "Moulin Rouge Hotel," *Wikipedia, the free encyclopedia,* p. 1.

25. Geran, *Beyond the Glimmering Light,* p. 121.

Chapter Four

1. Jerry Fink, "Not Forgotten," *Las Vegas Sun* (October 22, 2000), p. 6E.

2. Russell R. Elliot, with William D. Rowley, *History of Nevada,* 2nd ed. (Lincoln, Neb.: University of Nebraska Press, 1987), p. 393. It didn't matter to those in power that black citizens represented 10 percent of the Las Vegas population at the time. Blacks were still discriminated against in various white businesses and casino-hotels. See Janice R. Brooks, "The Proud Sounds of the Past Ring into the Future," *Las Vegas Magazine* (Spring 1996), p. 25.

3. *Ibid.* Prior to total segregation, some black stars and headliners were able to congregate, eat, sleep and gamble at the various hotel-casinos in Las Vegas where they performed. But with the onset of exclusionary Jim Crow policies, blacks were denied service in hotel-casinos and "a growing number of restaurants and stores as well." See Brooks, "Proud Sounds of the Past Ring into the Future," p. 25.

4. J.M. Kalil and Frank Curreri, "ATF agents will investigate blaze at Moulin Rouge," *Las Vegas Review-Journal* (May 30, 2003).

5. According to historian Steve Fischer, the Moulin Rouge would eventually have "a total of eight owners." Two majority owners were Louis Rubin and Al Bisno. The other owners included Tom Foley, Walter Zick, Larry Ouseley, Will Schwartz, Al Childs, and the hotel's casino boss, George Altman. In addition, there were seventeen unnamed investors in the Moulin Rouge, who were limited partners. See Steve Fischer. *When the Mob Ran Vegas: Stories of Money, Mayhem and Murder* (Boys Town, Neb.: Berkline Press, 2007), pp. 102–103.

6. Richard Todd, "Las Vegas, 'Tis of Thee," *The Atlantic Monthly* (February 2001), p. 102.

7. Roosevelt Fitzgerald, "Black Entertainers in Las Vegas: 1940–1960," unpublished paper in author's possession, p. 26.

8. Fink, "Not Forgotten," p. 6E.

9. Kalil and Curreri, "ATF agents will investigate blaze at Moulin Rouge," p.

10. Jay Tolson, "A History of Belief," *U.S. News & World Report* (November 26/December 3, 2007), p. 38.

11. Todd, "Las Vegas, 'Tis of Thee," p. 102.

12. *Ibid.*

13. Elliott, *History of Nevada,* p. 393.

14. John M. Findlay. *People of Chance: Gambling in American Society from Jamestown to Las Vegas* (New York: Oxford University Press, 1986), p. 191.

15. James Goodrich, "Negroes Can't Win in Las Vegas," p. 45.

16. Mary Frances Berry and John W. Blassingame. *Long Memory: The Black Experience in America* (New York: Oxford University Press, 1982), p. 384.

17. Findlay, *People of Chance,* p. 191.

18. Kalil and Curreri, "ATF agents will investigate blaze at Moulin Rouge," p. 4.

19. *Ibid.*, p. 5. Taylor's 1995 book, *Moulin Rouge Hotel History,* by Beehive Press, is not a history in the traditional sense at all, but is a hodge-podge of newspaper clippings, with some brief written notations. It excludes valuable information, particularly about the 1960s. In addition, Richard B. (Dick) Taylor is one of the many naysayers about the revival of the Moulin Rouge. He was once quoted as saying that rebuilding it wouldn't do any good. Another naysayer recently stated that "with the availability of neighborhood casinos, residents are unlikely to brave the Spaghetti Bowl traffic to travel to Bonanza Road, where day laborers seeking work and homeless people pushing shopping carts are common sights." See Michael Squires, "From Its Ashes: group buys historic site," *review-journal.com-News.*http://www.reviewjournal. com/lvrj _ home/2004/ Jan-29-Thu-2004/n.(1/15/2008), p. 1.

20. "Moulin Rouge Hotel History Book." http://www.lasvegashistorybooks.com/moulin.htm. (1/15/2008), p. 1. It has also been rumored that some of the residents of the Moulin Rouge were in the United States Witness Protection Program, but this contention has never been verified.

Chapter Five

1. Gary Dretzka, "Gambling on tradition," *Chicago Tribune* (February 6, 1996), p. 1.

2. William J. Wilson, "The Significance of Social and Racial Prisms," p. 401.

3. Shelby Steel, *White Guilt: How Blacks and Whites Together Destroyed the Promise of the Civil Rights Era* (New York: HarperCollins, 2006), p. 139.

4. Wilson, "The Significance of Social and Racial Prisms," p. 400.

5. Tom Flagg, "The Joint Jumped All Night," p. 11.

6. Wilson, "The Significance of Social and Racial Prisms," p. 396.

7. "History of the Moulin Rouge — Then and Now," *38th Year Birthday Celebration,* collectors' edition (May 21–23, 1993), p. 1.

8. "We Shall Overcome: Historic Places of the Civil Rights Movement — Moulin Rouge," p. 1.

9. Chuck Baker, "Moulin Rouge: Are the Lights Brighter on the Other Side of the Street?" *Las Vegas Magazine* (Spring, 1996), p. 27.

10. Mary M. Gafford, "Las Vegas' First Integrated Casino," p. 1.

11. *Ibid.*, p. 1.

12. Michael Green, "Moulin Rouge Hotel," *Nevada Online Encyclopedia*, http://www.onlinenevada.org/moulin_rouge, 12/16/2006, p. 1.

13. Moehring, *Resort City*, p. 184.

14. Gafford, "Las Vegas' First Integrated Casino," p. 1. According to Fischer, Foley was "licensed by the state of Nevada to operate the bar/tavern at the [Moulin] Rouge." See Steve Fischer. *When the Mob Ran Vegas*, p. 102.

15. Moehring, *Resort City*, p. 184.

16. Bracey, "The Moulin Rouge Mystique," p. 280. White residents near the hotel-casino also had serious concerns about the place and believed it would reduce their property values.

17. Moehring, *Resort City*, p. 184.

18. Elliot, "Moulin Rouge Hotel," p. 9.

19. "History of the Moulin Rouge — Then and Now," *38th Year Birthday Celebration*, p. 1.

20. Moehring, *Resort City*, p. 184.

21. Elliot, "Moulin Rouge Hotel," p. 9.

22. Bracey, "The Moulin Rouge Mystique," p. 281. During Leo Fry's ownership, the Moulin Rouge continued to run afoul of local laws.

23. Moehring, *Resort City*, p. 184.

24. Claytee D. White, "African American History in the West Vignette: The Moulin Rouge," http://faculty.washington.edu/qtaylor/aa_vignettes/org_moulin_rou, 12/16/2006, p. 2 (pp. 1–2).

Chapter Six

1. Earnest N. Bracey, "The Moulin Rouge Mystique," pp. 272–288.

2. Hal Rothman, *Neon Metropolis: How Las Vegas Started the Twenty-First Century* (New York: Routledge, 2002), p. 130.

3. Barbara Land and Myrick Land, *A Short History of Las Vegas*, 2nd ed. (Reno, Nev.: University of Nevada Press, 2004), p. 147.

4. Timothy Pratt, "Again, a Plan for Renewal," *Las Vegas Sun* (February 25, 2008), p. 2.

5. *Ibid.*

6. Constance Baker Motley. *Equal Justice under Law, an Autobiography* (New York: Farrar, Straus and Giroux, 1998), p. 246.

7. *Ibid.*

8. Mildred M. Wilson, "Entertain Them… But," in Stanley W. Paher, editor, *Nevada Towns & Tales, Volume II — South* (Las Vegas: Nevada Publications, 1982), p. 380.

9. Roosevelt Fitzgerald, "The Demographic Impact of Basic Magnesium Corporation on Southern Nevada," *Nevada Public Affairs Review*, 2 (1987), p. 33.

10. Janice R. Brooks, "The Proud Sounds of the Past Ring into the Future," p. 25.

11. Roy L. Brooks. *Integration or Separation? A Strategy for Racial Equality* (Cambridge, Mass.: Harvard University Press, 1996), pp. 2–3.

12. Rothman, *Neon Metropolis,* p. 130.

13. Eugene P. Moerhing, *Resort City*, p. 175.

14. Gary E. Elliott, "James B. McMillan: The Pursuit of Equality," in Richard O. Davies, editor, *The Maverick Spirit: Building the New Nevada* (Reno and Las Vegas: University of Nevada Press, 1999), p. 51.

15. Mary Frances Berry and John W. Blassingame, p. 105.

16. *Ibid.*, pp. 105–106.

17. *Ibid.*, pp. 106–107.

18. Dorraine A. Hooks, "Contributions of Black Theology," in James L. Conyers, Jr., and Alva P. Barnett, editors, *African American Sociology* (Chicago: Nelson-Hall Publishers, 1999), p. 98.

19. *Ibid.*

20. Larry Werner, "Black Pride: Rich Culture, History Legacy of Southern Nevada Black Community," pp. 1B-2B.

21. *Ibid.*, p. 2B.

22. Earnest N. Bracey, "The African Americans," in Jerry L. Simich and Thomas C. Wright, editors, *The Peoples of Las Vegas: One City, Many Faces* (Reno and Las Vegas: University of Nevada Press, 2005), p. 89.

23. Earnest N. Bracey, "Anatomy of Second Baptist Church: The First Black Baptist Church in Las Vegas," *Nevada Historical Society Quarterly*, Volume 43, Number 3 (Fall, 2000), pp. 201–213.

24. *Ibid.*

25. Motley, "Equal Justice under Law," p. 246.

Chapter Seven

1. Jos C. N. Raadschelders, *Government: A Public Administration Perspective* (Armonk, New York: M.E. Sharpe, 2003), p. 129.

2. Mary Frances Berry, *Black Resistance/White Law: A History of Constitutional Racism in America* (New York: Penguin Books, 1994), p. 166.

3. Clarence Ray, *Black Politics and Gaming in Las Vegas, 1920s–1980s*, as told to Helen M. Blue and Jamie Coughtry (Reno, Nev.: University of Nevada Oral History Program, 1991), p. 86.

4. *Ibid.*

5. *Ibid.*, pp. 86–87.

6. Gary Dretzka, "Gambling on tradition," *Chicago Tribune*, sec 5 (February 6, 1996), p. 2.

7. William J. Wilson, "The Significance of Social and Racial Prisms," p. 403.

8. Raadschelders, *Government: A Public Administration Perspective,* p. 129.

9. Berry, *Black Resistance/White Law,* p. 240.

10. Grant Sawyer, *Hang Tough! Grant Sawyer: an activist in the governor's mansion.* A narrative composed by R.T. King from interviews conducted by Gary E. Elliott (Reno, Nev.: University of Nevada Oral History Program, 1993), p. 99.

11. *Ibid.*

12. Dr. James B. McMillan. *Fighting Back: A Life in the Struggle for Civil Rights.* From oral history interviews conducted by Gary E. Elliott. A narrative interpretation by R.T. King (Reno, Nev.: University of Nevada Oral History Program, 1997), pp. 73–74.

13. Liz Benston, "Echelon Vegas blazes ahead toward 5,000 new rooms," *Las Vegas Sun* (July 7, 2007), p. 3.

14. McMillan, *Fighting Back,* pp. 94–95.

15. *Ibid.*, pp. 92–93. McMillan and other black activists read the riot act to city government officials, threatening marching and demonstrations on the Strip if integration didn't take place posthaste.

16. *Ibid.*, p. 92.

17. Woodrow Wilson. *Race, Community and Politics in Las Vegas, 1940–1980s.* An oral history conducted by Jamie Coughtry, edited by Jamie Coughtry and R.T. King (Reno, Nev.: University of Nevada Oral History Program, 1990), p. 85.

18. *Ibid.*

19. Sawyer, *Hang Tough!* p. 100.

20. McMillan, *Fighting Back,* pp. 97–98.

21. Wilson, *Race, Community and Politics in Las Vegas,* p. 85.

22. Lubertha Johnson, *Civil Rights Efforts in Las Vegas: 1940s–1960s.* An oral history conducted by Jamie Coughtry, edited by Jamie Coughtry and R. T. King (Reno, Nev.: University of Nevada Oral History Program, 1988), p. 64.

23. *Ibid.*

24. *Ibid.*

25. McMillan, *Fighting Back,* pp. 98.

26. *Ibid.*

Chapter Eight

1. "Moulin Rouge Hotel & Casino" flier dated 1990, p. 1.

2. Stokely Carmichael and Charles V. Hamilton, *Black Power: The Politics of Liberation in America* (New York: Vintage Books, 1967), p. 5.

3. Woodrow Wilson. *Race, Community and Politics in Las Vegas, 1940s-1980s,* p. 86. Note that Binion's Horseshoe was the only other hotel-casino that continued to close its biased doors, and discriminate against blacks in Las Vegas.

4. James B. McMillan. *Fighting Back,* p. 98.

5. David Brooks, "Despite promise of integration, self-imposed segregation persists," *Las Vegas Sun* (July 8, 2007), p. 5.

6. Langston Hughes, Milton Meltzer, C. Eric Lincoln, and Jon Michael Spencer. *A Pictorial History of African Americans,* 6th revised edition (New York: Crown Publishers, 1995), p. 363.

7. *Ibid.*, p. 405.

8. Norman Kelley, *The Head Negro in Charge Syndrome: The Dead End of Black Politics* (New York: Nation Books, 2004), p. 18.

9. Terry H. Anderson. *The Pursuit of Fairness: A History of Affirmative Action* (New York: Oxford University Press, 2004), p. 111.

10. Annelise Orleck. *Storming Caesars Palace,* p. 67.

11. Carmichael and Hamilton, *Black Power*, p. 125.

12. Eugene P. Moehring. *Resort City*, 2nd ed. (Reno and Las Vegas: University of Nevada Press, 2000), p. 188.

13. Anderson, *The Pursuit of Fairness*, p. 94.

14. Hughes *et al.*, *A Pictorial History of African Americans*, p. 405.

15. Carmichael and Hamilton, *Black Power*, p. 176.

16. Kelley, *The Head Negro in Charge Syndrome*, p. 18.

17. *Ibid.*

Chapter Nine

1. Gary Dretzka, "Gambling on tradition," Sec. 5, p. 3.

2. Langston Hughes, Milton Meltzer, C. Eric Lincoln, and Jon Michael Spencer. *A Pictorial History of African Americans,* p. 405.

3. Gunnar Myrdal. *An American Dilemma: The Negro Problem and Modern Democracy*, Volume 11 (New York: Pantheon Books, 1972), p. 624.

4. *Ibid.*

5. Ed Koch, "Breaking the rules when needed, he taught against prejudice," *Las Vegas Sun* (July 11, 2007), p. 2.

6. Larry Werner, "Black Pride: Rich culture, history legacy of Southern Nevada black community," p. 1B.

7. *Ibid.* See also Earnest N. Bracey, "Anatomy of Second Baptist Church," p. 201–13.

8. Harold Hyman and Bob Palm, "Black Las Vegans Forge Ahead Only to Fall Behind," *Las Vegas Sun* (1979), page number unknown.

9. *Ibid.*

10. Andrew L. Barlow. *Between Fear and Hope: Globalization and Race in the United States* (Lanham, Md.: Rowman & Littlefield Publishers, 2003), p. 38.

11. *Ibid.*

12. Werner, "Black Pride," p. 1B.

13. Harold Hyman and Bob Palm, "Many Black Hotel Workers Charge Loss of Jobs Due to the Color of Their Skin," *Las Vegas Sun* (1979), page number unknown.

14. *Ibid.*

15. *Ibid.* See also M.L. Miranda, *A History of Hispanics in Southern Nevada* (Reno and Las Vegas: University of Nevada Press, 1997), pp. 102–109.

16. *Ibid.*

17. *Ibid.*

18. "How Racism Affects the Mind — and Body," *The Wall Street Journal* (July 16, 2007), p. B5.

Chapter Ten

1. Perry Bruce Kaufman, "The Best City of Them All: A History of Las Vegas, 1930–1960," (Ph.D. dissertation, University of California, Santa Barbara, 1974), p. 21.

2. Sanford Wexler, *The Civil Rights Movement: An Eyewitness History, Introduction by Julian Bond* (New York: Facts On File, Inc., 1993), p. ix.

3. Gary E. Elliott, "James B. McMillan: The Pursuit of Equality," in Richard O. Davies, editor, *The Maverick Spirit: Building the New Nevada* (Reno and Las Vegas: University of Nevada Press, 1999), p. 50.

4. *Ibid.*

5. Elmer R. Rusco, "The Civil Rights Movement in Nevada," *Nevada Public Affairs Review* (1987), p. 78.

6. Nefretiti Makenta, "A View from West Las Vegas," in David Littlejohn, editor, *The Real Las Vegas: Life Beyond the Strip* (New York: Oxford University Press, 1999), p. 119.

7. Eugene P. Moehring. *Resort City*, p. 194.

8. Earnest N. Bracey, "A Shock to the System," *Las Vegas Life*, Vol. 2, No. 7, p. 56. According to journalist Alan Choate, the office of the long-defunct Clark County Legal Services was the location where "a lot of the organizing took place for the 1971 protest marches on the Strip [by Operation Life] decrying the state's treatment of welfare recipients, events that focused on a national spotlight on Nevada." See Alan Choate, "Moulin Rouge plan backed," *Las Vegas Review-Journal* (February 28, 2008), p. 2B.

9. Earnest N. Bracey, "The African Americans," in Jerry L. Simich and Thomas C. Wright, editors, *The Peoples of Las Vegas: One City, Many Faces* (Reno and Las Vegas: University of Nevada Press, 2005), p. 85

10. Makenta, "A View from West Las Vegas," p. 119. Clearly, there was a lot of heated activity stirring behind the scenes in the black community.

11. Harvard Sitkoff, *A New Deal for Blacks: The Emergence of Civil Rights as a National Issue: Volume I: The Depression Decade* (New York: Oxford University Press, 1978), p. 100.

12. Russell R. Elliott. *History of Nevada*, p. 393.

13. *Ibid.* Historian James W. Hulse tells us that Las Vegas had only 46,000 blacks in 1980, or 10 percent of the city's population. See James W. Hulse, *Forty Years in the Wilderness: Impressions of Nevada, 1940–1980* (Reno, Nev.: University of Nevada Press, 1986), p. 94. See also Albert Cameron Johns, *Nevada Politics*, 2nd edition (Dubuque, Iowa: Kendall/Hunt Publishing, 1976), p. 16.

14. Bracey, "The African Americans," p. 85.

15. Noralle Frankel, "Breaking the Chains: 1860–1880," in Robin D. G. Kelley and Earl Lewis, editors, *To Make Our World Anew: A History of African Americans* (New York: Oxford University Press, 2000), p. 276.

16. Earnest N. Bracey, "The Political Participation of Blacks in an Open Society: The Changing Political Climate in Nevada," *Nevada Historical Society Quarterly*, Vol. 42, No. 3 (Fall 1999), p. 140.

17. *Ibid.*, p. 141.

18. Bracey, "The African Americans," p. 86.

19. *Ibid.*

20. Makenta, "A View from West Las Vegas," p. 124. Both Hawkins and Brass lost their 1995 election bids to white politicians. James B. McMillan ran for city commissioner against Frank Hawkins, "a [former] All American fullback, and a professional football star with the Los Angeles Raiders," who proved to be a formidable foe and campaigner. McMillan lost the election. See Gary E. Elliott, "James B. McMillan: The Pursuit of Equality," p. 57.

21. Bracey, "The African Americans," p. 87.
22. *Ibid.*
23. Bracey, "The Political Participation of Blacks," p. 148.
24. Bracey, "The African Americans," p. 88.
25. Katherine Tate. *From Protest to Politics: The New Black Voters in American Elections* (New York: Russell Sage Foundation, 1993), p. 180.
26. *Ibid.*, p. 178.

Chapter Eleven

1. "Welcome to West Las Vegas," *Official Ethnic Destination and Visitors Guide* (Las Vegas Convention and Visitors Authority, 2000 edition), p. 35.
2. *Ibid.*
3. Robert Laxalt. *Nevada: A Bicentennial History* (Reno and Las Vegas: University of Nevada, 1977), p. 87.
4. Jamie Coughtry and R.T. King, editors, *Lubertha Johnson: Civil Rights Efforts in Las Vegas: 1940s-1960*, an oral history conducted by Jamie Coughtry (Reno, Nev.: University of Nevada Oral History Program, 1988), p. 39.
5. *Ibid.*
6. *Ibid.*
7. Jill Nelson, *Straight, No Chaser: How I became a Grown-Up Black Woman* (New York: Penguin Books, 1997), p. 16.
8. Annelise Orleck. *Storming Caesars Palace,* p. 2.
9. F. Chris Garcia, Christine Marie Sierra and Margaret Maier Murdock, "The Politics of Women and Ethnic Minorities," in Clive S. Thomas, editor, *Politics and Public Policy in Contemporary American West* (Albuquerque, N.M.: University of New Mexico Press, 1991), p. 212.
10. Jerry Fink, "Not Forgotten," *Las Vegas Sun* (October 22, 2000), p. 6E.
11. Chuck Barker, "Moulin Rouge: Are the Lights Brighter on the Other Side of the Street?," p. 26.
12. Jeff Simpson, "On how one troubled business was turned around — and why some might not be saved," *Las Vegas Sun* (March 9, 2008), p. 2. Note that $700 million is the estimated amount that the new developers are saying it will take to rebuild the Moulin Rouge hotel and casino. It is important to ask if the black neighborhood will also be revived.
13. Katherine Tate, *From Protest to Politics*, p. 15.
14. Garcia, Sierra, and Murdock, "The Politics of Women and Ethnic Minorities," p. 105.
15. Julianne Malveaux, "The 'lucky' world of black men?" *USA Today* (March 15, 2008), p. 13A.
16. *Ibid.*
17. Tate, "From Protest to Politics," p. 20.
18. "Welcome to West Las Vegas," p. 35.

Chapter Twelve

1. Dennis McBride, "Dam Days," *Nevada*, Vol. 55, No. 5 (September/October 1995), p. 13.
2. Albert Cameron Johns, *Nevada Politics*, p. 1.
3. *Ibid.*, p. 4.
4. Roosevelt Fitzgerald, "The Demographic Impact of Basic Magnesium Corporation on Southern Nevada," p. 33.
5. Thomas Moore, "Vegas is getting smarter, older," *Prime* (November 1996), p. 6.
6. Mickey Kaus. *The End of Equality* (New York: Basic Books, 1992), p. 116.
7. Joe William Trotter, Jr., ed., *The Great Migration in Historical Perspective: New Dimensions of Race, Class, and Gender* (Indianapolis: Indiana University Press, 1991), p. xii.
8. Larry Werner, "Black Pride: Rich Culture, History," p. 2B.
9. James W. Hulse, *Forty Years in the Wilderness: Impressions of Nevada, 1940–1980* (Reno, Nev.: University of Nevada Press, 1986), p. 91.
10. John M. Findlay. *People of Chance*, p. 189.
11. *Ibid.*, p. 191.
12. *Ibid.*
13. Fitzgerald, "The Demographic Impact of Basic Magnesium Corporation on Southern Nevada," p. 34.
14. Findlay, *People of Chance*, p. 190. A 1996 article in the *Las Vegas Review-Journal* said that according to past government statistics, home loans for minorities in Nevada increased by more than 80 percent. See "Minority Home Loans Up Sharply Across U.S.," *Las Vegas Review-Journal* (October 31, 1996), p. 31.
15. Findlay, "People of Chance," p. 31. Today, black people "reside in all areas of the [Las Vegas] valley and within all social strata of Las Vegas, making the black Diaspora as diverse as Las Vegas itself." See "Welcome to West Las Vegas," p. 35.
16. Werner, "Black Pride," p. 2B.
17. Eugene P. Moehring. *Resort City*, p. 189.
18. Elmer Rusco, "The Civil Rights Movement in Nevada," *Nevada Public Affairs Review*, No. 2 (1987), p. 75.
19. Werner, "Black Pride," p. 2B.
20. Fitzgerald, "The Demographic Impact of Basic Magnesium Corporation on Southern Nevada," p. 33.
21. Michael W. Bowers, *The Sagebrush State: Nevada's History, Government and Politics* (Reno and Las Vegas: University of Nevada Press, 1996), p. 34.
22. Russell R. Elliott, *History of Nevada*, p. 393.
23. Findlay, *People of Chance*, p. 191.
24. Woodrow Wilson, *Race, Community and Politics in Las Vegas, 1940s–1980s*, p. 100.
25. Findlay, *People of Chance*, p. 191.
26. Werner, "Black Pride," p. 2B. There was also the short-lived Enterprise Community Federal Credit Union, which boasted that it was "eligible to receive as much as $1.5 million in non-member deposits from banks, casinos and other businesses

under federal law." But it too was unable to survive in the struggling financial market. See John G. Edwards, "Credit Union Created to Serve Poor Areas," *Las Vegas Review-Journal and Las Vegas Sun* (January 12, 1997), p. 1F.

27. "In This Era of Megamergers, Community Banks Thrive," *Las Vegas Review-Journal* (October 4, 1996), p. 3D. Large banks, however, "complain that credit unions don't pay income taxes, like commercial banks," which they considered unfair. See Jennifer Brown, "Credit Union Seeking Federal Help," *Las Vegas Review-Journal and Las Vegas Sun* (November 2, 1996), p. 1.

28. Lubertha Johnson, *Civil Rights Efforts in Las Vegas: 1940–1960s*, p. 52.

29. *Ibid.*

30. *Ibid.* Unfortunately, the million dollars that Johnson claimed was in the Westside Credit Union from her business cannot be verified.

31. Woodrow Wilson, *Race, Community and Politics in Las Vegas, 1940s-1980s* pp. 98–99. Members of the Westside Federal Credit Union shared a common bond with all of the other members by being members of the NAACP.

32. *Ibid.*, p. 100.

Chapter Thirteen

1. Earnest N. Bracey, "The Moulin Rouge Mystique," p. 283.

2. Langston Hughes, Milton Meltzer, C. Eric Lincoln, and Jon Michael Spencer. *A Pictorial History of African Americans*, p. 405.

3. Bracey, "The Moulin Rouge Mystique," p. 283.

4. *Ibid.*

5. "Hotel Gets Drop In Property Tax," *Las Vegas Sun* (January 15, 1976), page number unknown.

6. *Ibid.*

7. *Ibid.*

8. John Crowe, "Blaze at Moulin Rouge: Screaming Teens Flee Hotel Fire," *Las Vegas Review-Journal* (July 14, 1966), page number unknown.

9. "Moulin Rouge Offered to County as Hospital," *Las Vegas Sun* (January 10, 1968), page number unknown.

10. *Ibid.* According to Harry Miller, once the receiver for the Moulin Rouge, the Atomic Energy Commission considered taking over the hotel-casino for office space, but that never materialized. See "AEC May Lease Rouge," *Las Vegas Sun* (September 26, 1956), page number unknown.

11. "Writ Re-Opens License Fight on Hideaway," *Las Vegas Sun* (November 13, 1968), page number unknown.

12. *Ibid.*

13. "Race Spat to Board," *Las Vegas Review-Journal* (October 13, 1963), p. 2.

14. *Ibid.*

15. "Racial Bias Meeting Held," *Las Vegas Sun* (October 14, 1963), page number unknown.

16. Donald Warman, "Commission Hears Moulin Rouge Issue," *Las Vegas Review-Journal* (October 17, 1963), pp. 1–2.

17. Crowe, "Blaze at Moulin Rouge," p. 1.

18. *Ibid.* One hysterical teenage girl, "climbed through a ground floor window, [and] was cut by broken glass." See "Fire Chases Guests from Moulin Rouge," *Las Vegas Sun* (June 15, 1956), page number unknown.

19. *Ibid.*

20. "$775,000 Damage Suit Filed Against LV Hotel," *Las Vegas Sun* (February 7, 1968), page number unknown.

21. "City Files Suit Against Hotel," *Las Vegas Sun* (May 4, 1976), page number unknown.

22. *Ibid.* The Moulin Rouge also had to correct city fire code violations in 1977, stemming from injuries suffered by Shirley Roy, 58, a resident who was struck "when part of a ceiling fell on her, due to leakage from recent rains." She was later treated at Southern Nevada Memorial Hospital, and released. City fire inspectors told managers at the Moulin Rouge "to correct the problems or face closure." See "Hotel has corrected violations," *Las Vegas Sun* (October 3, 1977), page number unknown.

23. "Bob Bailey rally set at hotel," *Las Vegas Sun* (April 15, 1971), page number unknown.

24. *Ibid.*

25. Harold Hyman and Bob Palm, "Many Black Hotel Workers Charge Loss of Jobs Due to the Color of Their Skin," *Las Vegas Sun* (1979), page number unknown.

26. Earnest N. Bracey, "Ruby Duncan, Operation Life, and Welfare Rights in Nevada," *Nevada Historical Society Quarterly*, Volume 44, No. 2 (Summer 2001), p. 140.

27. *Ibid.*

28. Dick Odessky, "New lease on life for Moulin Rouge," *Las Vegas Sun* (January 5, 1977), page number unknown.

29. *Ibid.*

30. *Ibid.*

31. Dick Odessky, "New lease on life for Moulin Rouge." Also see "Moulin Rouge Hotel Awaits Reopening," *Las Vegas Sun* (March 8, 1977), page number unknown.

32. "Moulin Rouge Hotel Awaits Reopening."

Chapter Fourteen

1. Dick Odessky, "New lease on life for Moulin Rouge," *Las Vegas Sun* (January 5, 1977), page number unknown. Odessky also pointed out that the Roys had come to Las Vegas in "hopes of buying Echo Bay at Lake Mead, from Argent Corp. But the deal fell through."

2. *Ibid.*

3. *Ibid.*

4. *Ibid.*

5. "Moulin Rouge Hotel Awaits Reopening," *Las Vegas Sun* (February 8, 1977), page number unknown.

6. Odessky, "New lease on life for Moulin Rouge."

7. "Moulin Rouge Hotel Awaits Reopening."

8. *Ibid.* By that time the showroom had remained closed for more than 22 years. See also Gary E. Elliott, "Moulin Rouge Hotel," p. 8 and p. 13.

9. Odessky, "New lease on life for Moulin Rouge."
10. *Ibid.*
11. Earnest N. Bracey, "The Moulin Rouge Mystique," p. 283.
12. *38th Year Birthday Celebration Bulletin*, p. 2.
13. *Ibid.*
14. *Ibid.*
15. Kristi Goodwin, "Putting A New Face On The Past," *Las Vegas Style* (November 1992), p. 16 and p. 25.
16. Robin Jenkins, "Moulin Rouge to Reopen," *Indian Voices* (January 1993), p. 3.
17. Frank Wright, "The Late, Late Show," *Nevada* (May-June 1993), p. 17.
18. *38th Year Birthday Celebration Bulletin*, p. 2.
19. Larry Werner, "Black Pride," p. 1-B.
20. *Ibid.*
21. Lerone Bennett, Jr. *The Shaping of Black America: The Struggles and Triumphs of African-Americans, 1519 to the 1990s* (New York: Penguin Group, 1993), p. 292.
22. *38th Year Birthday Celebration Bulletin*, p. 2.

Chapter Fifteen

1. Timothy Pratt, "Again, a Plan for Renewal," *Las Vegas Sun* (February 25, 2008), p. 2.
2. Gary E. Elliott, "James B. McMillan: The Pursuit of Equality," p. 55.
3. Alan Choate, "West Las Vegas ready for economic revival," *Las Vegas Review-Journal* (February 24, 2008), p. 9B. The Moulin Rouge is east of Martin Luther King Boulevard, and the area that surrounds the 19-acre site is still dotted by burned-out and vacant buildings and "a United Parcel Service distribution center and a homeless shelter." See Benjamin Spillman, "Moulin Rouge taps Epic Gaming," *Las Vegas Review Journal* (March 6, 2008), p. 3D.
4. *Ibid.*
5. Sonya Padgett, "Next step for civil rights," *Las Vegas Review-Journal* (January 20, 2008), p. J4.
6. Choate, "West Las Vegas ready for economic revival," p. 9B.
7. *Ibid.*
8. Benjamin Spillman, "Backers pitch redevelopment of neglected Moulin Rouge," *Las Vegas Review-Journal* (February 26, 2008), p. 1D.
9. Pratt, "Again, a Plan for Renewal," p. 2.
10. Clarence Page, "Blacks left behind despite changes in nation since the civil rights era," *Las Vegas Sun* (July 29, 2007), p. 6.
11. Harold L. Wolman and Norman C. Thomas, "Black Interests, Black Groups, and Black Influence in the Federal Policy Process: The Cases of Housing and Education," *The Journal of Politics*, Vol. 32 (1970), p. 894.
12. James K. Galbraith, *Created Unequal: The Crisis in American Pay* (Chicago: University of Chicago Press, 2000), p. 7.
13. James W. Hulse, *The Silver State: Nevada's Heritage Reinterpreted* (Reno and Las Vegas: University of Nevada Press, 1991), p. 308.

14. *Ibid.*, pp. 309–310.

15. Tamara Henry, "School's Out for Assumptions: Many poor, minority students Out-Achieve Wealthy Districts," *USA Today* (December 13, 2001), p. 10D.

16. Doug Smith, "Agassi gives all of himself on, off tennis court," *USA Today* (August 31, 2001), p. 8C.

17. Ruth Sidel, *Battling Bias: The Struggle for Identity and Community on College Campuses* (New York: Penguin Books, 1994), p. 51.

18. Clark County School District Brochure, Board of School Trustees (1995), p. 1.

19. Natalie Patton, "Clark County School Board, District C," *Las Vegas Review-Journal* (August 28, 1996), p. 22F.

20. Nichole Davis, "Incumbents Focus on Unfinished Business," *The Las Vegas Sentinel-Voice*, Vol. 17, Issue 7 (June 20, 1996), p. 13.

21. Natalie Patton, "Clark County School Board," p. 22F.

Chapter Sixteen

1. *38th Year Birthday Celebration Bulletin*, p. 2.

2. John Hope Franklin, "History of Racial Segregation in the United States," *Annals of the American Academy of Political and Social Science*, Vol. 34 (March 1956), p. 1.

3. Kristi Goodwin, "Putting A New Face On The Past," p. 24.

4. Earnest N. Bracey, "The Moulin Rouge Mystique," p. 283.

5. *38th Year Birthday Celebration Bulletin*, p. 2.

6. Joanne Goodwin, "Sarann Knight-Preddy," *Nevada Online Encyclopedia*, http://www.onlinenevada.org/sarann_knight_preddy,_entrepreneur, p. 2.

7. *Ibid.* Sarann Knight-Preddy was the first black person to own a gaming license in Nevada. When she bought the Lincoln Bar for blacks in Hawthorne, it was renamed the Tonga Club.

8. Helen M. Blue and Jamie Coughtry. *Clarence Ray: Black Politics and Gaming in Las Vegas, 1920s–1980s* (Reno, Nev.: University of Nevada Oral History Program, 1991), p. 87.

9. Goodwin, "Putting a New Face on the Past," p. 24.

10. *Ibid.*

11. Bracey, "The Moulin Rouge Mystique," p. 283.

12. Goodwin, "Sarann Knight-Preddy," pp. 1–2.

13. Gary Dretzka, "Gambling on tradition," *Chicago Tribune* (February 6, 1996), sec 5, p. 3.

14. Joan Shepard, "City Council Approves W.L.V. Economic Development Plans," *Las Vegas Sentinel Voice*, Volume 13, Issue 20 (September 10, 1992), p. 1.

15. *Ibid.*

16. *Ibid.*

17. Marian Green, "Moulin Rouge denied grant," *Las Vegas Review-Journal* (November 16, 1995), p. 1B.

18. Caren Benjamin, "Historic Moulin Rouge's luck may have run out for good," *Las Vegas Review-Journal* (November 26, 1996), p. 1B.

19. *Ibid.*, p. 2B.

20. *38th Year Birthday Celebration Bulletin,* p. 2.

21. Shepard, "City Council Approves W.L.V. Economic Development plans," p. 1.

22. Frank Wright, "The Late, Late Show," *Nevada* (May-June 1993), p. 17.

23. Steve Sebelius, "Moulin Rouge will get $3 mil. city loan," *Las Vegas Sun* (March 7, 1996), p. 3B.

24. *Ibid.*

25. *Ibid.*

26. *Ibid.*

Chapter Seventeen

1. Lerone Bennett, Jr. *The Shaping of Black America,* p. 292.

2. *38th Year Birthday Celebration,* p. 2. The Black Chamber of Commerce of Las Vegas is now called The Las Vegas Urban Chamber of Commerce.

3. Caren Benjamin, "Historic Moulin Rouge's luck may have run out for good," *Las Vegas Review-Journal* (November 26, 1996), p. 2B.

4. *Ibid.* More than ever, Sarann Knight-Preddy and her family lobbied the city of Las Vegas for grants and loans to reinvent the Moulin Rouge. But alas, their seemingly solid plan failed to gain traction.

5. Interview by author with Sarann Knight-Preddy, October 15, 1996, at the offices of the Moulin Rouge.

6. Marian Green, "Moulin Rouge denied grant," *Las Vegas Review-Journal* (November 16, 1995), p. 1B.

7. *Ibid.*, p. 2B.

8. *Ibid.*

9. David McGrath Schwartz, "Historic building unwrapped," *Las Vegas Review-Journal* (July 3, 2007), p. 2B. Note that $3.6 million has already been spent on the post office's renovation. According to journalist Schwartz, the money ($3.6 million) for the project, which will eventually "cost upward of $30 million," was provided "by the state Historic Preservation Office ... the National Park Service, the State Commission for Cultural Affairs and the Las Vegas Centennial Commission."

10. Marian Green, "Pequots eye Las Vegas," *Las Vegas Review-Journal* (April 19, 1996), p. 1A. See also Caren Benjamin, "Historic Moulin Rouge's luck may have run out for good," p. 2B).

11. *Ibid.*, p. 3A. Some have claimed that the Pequot tribe members were disingenuous in wanting to invest in the Moulin Rouge at this time, but that still remains to be seen.

12. Clarence Page, "Blacks left behind despite changes in nation since the civil rights era," *Las Vegas Sun* (July 29, 2007), p. 6.

13. Green, "Pequots eye Las Vegas," p. 3A.

14. Green, "Moulin Rouge denied grant," p. 2B.

15. Tanya Flanagan, "Return of the Rouge," *Las Vegas Review-Journal* (February 13, 1998), p. 6B.

16. *Ibid.*

17. Kevin Boyle, "Urban crisis still smoldering," *Las Vegas Review-Journal* (August 1, 2007), p. 9B.

18. Flanagan, "Return of the Rouge," p. 1B.

Chapter Eighteen

1. Joseph N. Browley, "Race and Residence: The Politics of Open Housing in Nevada," *Sagebrush and Neon: Studies in Nevada Politics*, Eleanore Bushnell, editor (Reno, Nev.: University of Nevada Bureau of Governmental Research, 1973), p. 73.

2. *Ibid.*

3. James W. Hulse. *The Silver State*, p. 310.

4. Tanya Flanagan, "Return of the Rouge," p. 6B.

5. *Ibid.*

6. *Ibid.* Bart Maybie bought all the properties around the Moulin Rouge, to get "control of the illegal activities ... and make people feel safer going to the casino." See Michael Squires, "Restoration planned for Moulin Rouge," *Las Vegas Review-Journal* (March 21, 2001), p. 10B.

7. *Ibid.*

8. *Ibid.* Flamboyant gaming entrepreneur Bob Stupak also tried to make a deal with Bart Maybie for revamping the Moulin Rouge, but the transaction was never finalized between the two businessmen. See Gary Thompson, "Stupak looks at Moulin Rouge makeover," *Las Vegas Sun* (May 26, 1999), pp. 3C-4C.

9. *Ibid.*

10. *Ibid.*

11. Informational and donation flier, "The Historic Moulin Rouge Preservation Association, Inc.," 1996, p. 1.

12. *Ibid.* Eventually, Sarann Knight-Preddy, who owned the Moulin Rouge from 1985 to 1997, wanted "to put the story of the Moulin Rouge on stage, as a musical, and then to turn the production into a movie." Sarann Knight-Preddy collaborated with playwright Dianna Saffold on this venture, with a goal "to take the show on the road and ultimately to Broadway and Hollywood." See Jerry Fink, "Not Forgotten," *Las Vegas Sun* (October 22, 2000), p. 6E.

13. Jen Lawson, "Some features of Moulin Rouge salvageable," *Las Vegas Sun* (June 5, 2003), p. 1B. Duncan applied for a $1 million America's Treasures grant in May 2003, but lost eligibility because of the later destruction of the Moulin Rouge by fire.

14. Tiffannie Bond, "Losing a bit of history," *Summerlin View* (June 11, 2003), p. 3AA. Duncan, originally from Arkansas and born on a former slave plantation, also wholeheartedly believed in preserving the legacy of the Moulin Rouge, so that, as she put it, a "history of achievement can be told." Some reports mistakenly spell Katherine Duncan's name as Katherine Dunn.

15. Ed Koch, "Blaze is latest chapter in hotel's storied history," *Las Vegas Sun* (May 29, 2003), p. 94.

16. Lawson, "Some features of Moulin Rouge salvageable," p. 1B.

17. *Ibid.*

18. Koch, "Blaze is latest chapter in hotel's storied history," p. 9A. The Moulin

Rouge hotel and casino, fortunately, "had been closed and undergoing renovation when the fire occurred." It was claimed that Fred Lewis Ball, a black man called "Bubba," was responsible for starting the fire. See "Moulin Rouge Casino Fire in Las Vegas Was Arson, Authorities Say," *Las Vegas Now*, 2003, http://www.lasvegasnow.com/Global/story.asp?5=1299079 (1/15/2008 2:17PM), p. 4.

19. Ed Koch, "Historic casino faces challenges," *Las Vegas Sun* (May 28, 2005), p. 16B.

20. Hubble Smith, "Moulin Rouge renovation in Limbo," *Las Vegas Review-Journal* (July 10, 2004), p. 1D.

Chapter Nineteen

1. Hubble Smith, "Moulin Rouge renovation in limbo," p. 1D.

2. John L. Smith, "Moulin Rouge finally succumbs to slow burn of felonious neglect," *Las Vegas Review-Journal* (June 1, 2003), p. B1.

3. Jace Radke and Jen Lawson, "Fire ravages historic Moulin Rouge casino," *Las Vegas Sun* (May 29, 2003), p. 9A.

4. Ed Koch, "Historic casino faces challenges," *Las Vegas Sun* (May 28, 2005), p. 16B.

5. John L. Smith, "Moulin Rouge finally succumbs to slow burn of felonious neglect," p. B1.

6. Tiffannie Bond, "Losing a bit of history," *Summerlin View* (June 11, 2003), p. 4AA.

7. *Ibid.*, p. 3AA.

8. Hubble Smith, "Moulin Rouge renovation in limbo," p. 1D. The appeal of the place was always deep, especially for blacks living in Las Vegas.

9. *Ibid.*, pp. 1D and 6D.

10. *Ibid.*

11. *Ibid.*

12. *Ibid.* The new black owners have the intensity and drive to realize their dream of building a totally new Moulin Rouge. The black owners also know that they have to exceed expectations.

13. Jim Myers. *Afraid of the Dark: What Whites and Blacks Need to Know About Each Other* (Chicago, Ill.: Lawrence Hill Books, 2000), p. 345.

14. *Ibid.*, p. 324.

15. Charles W. Mills. *Blackness Visible: Essays on Philosophy and Race* (Ithaca, N.Y. and London: Cornell University Press, 1998), p. 165.

16. Michael W. Bowers. *The Sagebrush State*, p. 35.

17. Earnest N. Bracey, "The African Americans," *The Peoples of Las Vegas: One City, Many Faces*, edited by Terry L. Simich and Thomas C. Wright (Reno and Las Vegas: University of Nevada Press, 2005), p. 92.

18. *Ibid.*, p. 93.

19. "New $2.5 billion mega-resort planned," *Nevada Contractor* (June 2007), p. 7.

20. *Ibid.* According to black developer Donahue Peeble, the initial hotel tower will open by 2009.

21. Sean Whaley, "Group lists endangered sites," *Las Vegas Review-Journal* (May 15, 2004), p. 2B. The Moulin Rouge's landmark status did not save it from burning, but the place "could still be preserved."

22. Timothy Pratt, "Story changes, squalor doesn't," *Las Vegas Sun* (April 6, 2007), p. 3.

23. *Ibid.* The plan should be to raze the old hotel-apartments at the place, to make room for a new Moulin Rouge.

24. "Palms Casino Resort," *Wikipedia, the free encyclopedia*, http://en.wikipedia.org/wiki/Palms_Casino_Resort, p. 1. Many neighborhood casinos point to the Palms Casino and its phenomenal success. The Maloof family (Joe, George, Gavin and Phil) currently owns the Palms.

25. Geoff Schumacher, "North Las Vegas can't escape Sin City," *Las Vegas Review-Journal* (September 24, 2006), p. 3D. Many strip bosses may believe that off-Strip casinos are still bad for their business, because of their quaint competitiveness and proximity.

26. Timothy Pratt, "January cold snap claimed squatter," *Las Vegas Sun* (March 6, 2007), p. 1.

27. *Ibid.*

28. *Ibid.*

29. *Ibid.*

30. *Ibid.*

Chapter Twenty

1. Steve Fischer. *When the Mob Ran Vegas*, p. 102.

2. Tony Illia, "Moulin Rouge makeover moves forward," *Business Press* (December 3, 2007), p. 3.

3. *Ibid.* See also Dick Taylor, *Moulin Rouge — Hotel History* (Beehive Press, 1995).

4. Jearold Winston Holland, *Black Recreation: A Historical Perspective* (Chicago: Burnham Inc., Publishers, 2002), p. 156.

5. *Ibid.*

6. Fischer, *When the Mob Ran Vegas*, p. 102.

7. Holland, *Black Recreation*, p. 157.

8. *Ibid.*

9. Fischer, *When the Mob Ran Vegas*, p. 107. According to Fischer, "the place was coming apart at the seams with business," p. 109.

10. Holland, *Black Recreation*, p. 157

11. *Ibid.*, p . 198.

12. Fischer, *When the Mob Ran Vegas*, p. 109. Compared with some of the fabulous specialty and exclusive showrooms at the now-defunct Sands, the Dunes, and the New Frontier, as Fischer tells us, the former Café Rouge "was the only showroom in Las Vegas that was continuously selling out," p. 109. At any rate, is there any way to definitively find out if the original owners stealthily and criminally took money and pocketed it from "the soft count room at the Moulin Rouge?" Probably not. So we can only speculate. Unfortunately, as professor of history Michael Green tells us, "the Moulin Rouge was a victim of its own [limited] success," because it was never seen as

profitable. See Michael Green, "Backstory: Requiem for the Rouge," *Las Vegas Mercury* (June 5, 2003), page number unknown.

13. Ollie A. Johnson III and Karin L. Stanford, editors, *Black Political Organizations in the Post-Civil Rights Era* (New Brunswick, N.J.: Rutgers University Press, 2002), p. 4.

14. Fischer, *When the Mob Ran Vegas*, p. 103.

15. *Ibid.*

16. *Ibid.*

17. Johnson and Stanford, *Black Political Organizations*, p. 7.

18. Fischer, *When the Mob Ran Vegas*, p. 110.

Conclusion

1. "The New Vegas," *Cigar Aficionado* (March/April 2006), p. 64.

2. Kim Clark, "Against the Odds," *U.S. News & World Report* (May 23, 2006), p. 47. Some Las Vegans are getting more and more cynical about the building boom taking place in Las Vegas. Is the city over-saturated with hotels and casinos already with future potential for a hotel glut?

3. "The New Vegas," p. 64. According to journalist Tony Illia, it takes an experienced, well-financed development team to enter the market in Las Vegas. And this would certainly be needed if a new high-rise Moulin Rouge hotel and casino is finally built at the old site. It would also mean that the black owners would have to line up financing for a fast-paced venture, in a volatile market. See Tony Illia, "Pinnacle Las Vegas again changes contractors," in the *Business Press* (September 10, 2007), p. 2.

4. Clark, "Against the Odds," p. 47.

5. Carri Geer Thevenot, "Ex-wife claims Moulin Rouge executive owes child support," *Las Vegas Review-Journal* (April 9, 2007), p. 9B. The new black principals truly believe that a new Moulin Rouge could become a symbol of revitalization on Westside.

6. *Ibid.*, p. 9B.

Postscript

1. Benjamin Spillman, "Moulin Rouge gets another go," *Las Vegas Review-Journal* (October 5, 2007), p. 1D.

2. Michael Squires, "Group buys historic site," *Las Vegas Review-Journal* (January 29, 2004), pp. 1B and 6B.

3. Spillman, "Moulin Rouge gets another go," p. 1D.

4. Tony Illia, "Moulin Rouge makeover moves forward," *Business Press* (December 3, 2007), p. 3.

5. Spillman, "Moulin Rouge gets another go," p. 1D.

6. *Ibid.* Despite skepticism by casino industry experts and academic researchers, it remains to be seen if the Moulin Rouge will be a financial success, when the place is finally rebuilt. Some other features planned for the redeveloped Moulin Rouge will include "40,000 square feet of meeting and convention space, a 1,500-seat showroom and a bar," as well as "a botanical atrium, a cultural center, four restaurants and a beauty

salon." See Tony Illia, "Moulin Rouge makeover moves forward," *Business Press* (December 3, 2007), p. 3.

7. *Ibid.* As already pointed out in this story, the mundane activities, or the day-to-day operations of the Moulin Rouge are not explored or investigated in this work.

8. Squires, "Group buys historic site," p. 1B.

9. Spillman, "Moulin Rouge gets another go," p. 1D. Construction is set to begin at the Moulin Rouge site after all the old buildings are leveled.

10. Tony Illia, "Moulin Rouge makeover moves forward," p. 3. The Moulin Rouge, as Illia tells us, "may get a breath of new life now that a development is in place between its current owner[s] and a Fairfax, Virginia-based [finance] company."

11. *Ibid.*

Bibliography

Anderson, Terry H. *The Pursuit of Fairness: A History of Affirmative Action.* New York: Oxford University Press, 2004.

Baker, Chuck. "Moulin Rouge: Are the Lights Brighter on the Other Side of the Street?" *Las Vegas Magazine,* Spring 1996.

Barlow, Andrew L. *Between Fear and Hope: Globalization and Race in the United States.* Lanham, Md: Rowman & Littlefield Publishers, 2003.

Benjamin, Caren. "Historic Moulin Rouge's luck may have run out for good," *Las Vegas Review-Journal,* November 26, 1996.

Bennett, Lerone, Jr. *The Shaping of Black America: The Struggles and Triumphs of African-Americans, 1519 to the 1990s.* New York: Penguin Group, 1993.

Benston, Liz. "Echelon Vegas blazes ahead toward 5,000 new rooms," *Las Vegas Sun,* July 7, 2007.

Berry, Mary Frances. *Black Resistance/White Law: A History of Constitutional Racism in America.* New York: Penguin Books, 1994.

_____, and John W. Blassingame. *Long Memory: The Black Experience in America.* New York: Oxford University Press, 1982.

Best, Katherine, and Katherine Hillyer. *Las Vegas: Play Town U.S.A.* New York: David McKay, 1955.

"Bob Bailey rally set at hotel," *Las Vegas Sun,* April 15, 1971.

Bond, Tiffannie. "Losing a bit of history," *Summerlin View,* June 11, 2003.

Bowers, Michael W. *The Sagebrush State: Nevada's History, Government, and Politics,* 2nd ed. Reno and Las Vegas: University of Nevada Press, 2002.

Boyle, Kevin. "Urban crisis still smoldering," *Las Vegas Review-Journal,* August 1, 2007.

Bracey, Earnest N. "The African Americans," *The Peoples of Las Vegas: One City, Many Faces,* ed. Terry L. Simich and Thomas C. Wright. Reno and Las Vegas: University of Nevada Press, 2005.

_____. "Anatomy of Second Baptist Church: The First Black Baptist Church in Las Vegas," *Nevada Historical Society Quarterly,* Volume 43, Number 3 (Fall, 2000).

_____. "The Migration of Blacks to Las Vegas," in Steven A. Reich, ed., *Encyclopedia of the Great Black Migration,* Volume 1: A-L. Westport, Conn.: Greenwood Press, 2006.

_____. "The Moulin Rouge Mystique: Blacks and Equal Rights in Las Vegas," *Nevada Historical Society Quarterly,* Vol. 39, No. 4 (Winter 1996).

_____. "The Political Participation of Blacks in an Open Society: The Changing Political Climate in Nevada," *Nevada Historical Society Quarterly*, Vol. 42, No. 3 (Fall 1999).

_____. "Ruby Duncan, Operation Life, and Welfare Rights in Nevada," *Nevada Historical Society Quarterly*, Volume 44, No. 2 (Summer 2001).

_____. "A Shock to the System," *Las Vegas Life*, Vol. 2, No. 7.

Brooks, David. "Despite promise of integration, self-imposed segregation persists," *Las Vegas Sun*, July 8, 2007.

Brooks, Janice R. "The Proud Sounds of the Past Ring into the Future," *Las Vegas Magazine*, Spring, 1996.

Brooks, Roy L. *Integration or Separation? A Strategy for Racial Equality.* Cambridge: Harvard University Press, 1996.

Browley, Joseph. "Race and Residence: the Politics of Open Housing in Nevada." In *Sagebrush and Neon: Studies in Nevada Politics*, edited by Eleanore Bushnell. Reno: University of Nevada Bureau of Governmental Research, 1973.

Brown, Jennifer. "Credit Union Seeking Federal Help," *Las Vegas Review-Journal and Las Vegas Sun*, November 2, 1996.

Carmichael, Stokely, and Charles V. Hamilton. *Black Power: The Politics of Liberation in America.* New York: Vintage Books, 1967.

"City Files Suit Against Hotel," *Las Vegas Sun*, May 4, 1976.

Clark County School District Brochure. Board of School Trustees, 1995.

Clark, Kim. "Against the Odds," *U.S. News & World Report*, May 23, 2006.

Choate, Alan. "West Las Vegas ready for economic revival," *Las Vegas Review-Journal*, February 24, 2008.

Coughtry, Jamie, and R.T. King. *Woodrow Wilson: Race, Community and Politics in Las Vegas, 1940s–1980s.* Reno: University of Nevada Press Oral History Program, 1990.

Crowe, John. "Blaze at Moulin Rouge: Screaming Teens Flee Hotel Fire," *Las Vegas Review-Journal*, July 14, 1966.

Davis, Nichole. "Incumbents Focus on Unfinished Business," *The Las Vegas Sentinel-Voice*, Vol. 17, Issue 7 (June 20, 1996).

Dretzka, Gary. "Gambling on Tradition," *Chicago Tribune*, February 6, 1996.

Edwards, John G. "Credit Union Created to Serve Poor Areas," *Las Vegas Review-Journal and Las Vegas Sun*, January 12, 1997.

Elliott, Gary E. "James B. McMillan: The Pursuit of Equality." In *The Maverick Spirit: Building the New Nevada,* edited by Richard O. Davies. Reno and Las Vegas: University of Nevada Press, 1999.

_____. "The Moulin Rouge Hotel: A Critical Appraisal of a Las Vegas Legend," unpublished paper in possession of the author.

Elliott, Russell, with William D. Rowley. *History of Nevada*, 2nd ed. Lincoln: University of Nebraska Press, 1987.

Findlay, John M. *People of Chance: Gambling in America Society from Jamestown to Las Vegas*, New York: Oxford University Press, 1986.

Fink, Jerry. "Not Forgotten," *Las Vegas Sun*, October 22, 2000.

Fischer, Steve. *When the Mob Ran Vegas: Stories of Money, Mayhem and Murder.* Boys Town, Neb.: Berkline Press, 2007.

Fitzgerald, Roosevelt. "Black Entertainers in Las Vegas: 1940–1960," unpublished paper in possession of the author.

_____. "The Demographic Impact of Basic Magnesium Corporation on Southern Nevada," *Nevada Public Affairs Review*, No. 2 (1987).

Flagg, Tom. "The Joint Jumped All Night: The Moulin Rouge: Harbinger of Integration in Las Vegas," *Oasis: The Magazine of the University of Nevada, Las Vegas*, Autumn 1991.

Flanagan, Tanya. "Return of the Rouge," *Las Vegas Review-Journal*, February 13, 1998.

Franklin, John Hope. "History of Racial Segregation in the United States," *Annals of the American Academy of Political and Social Science*, Vol. 34 (March 1956).

Gafford, Mary M. "Las Vegas' First Integrated Casino," *Las Vegas Centennial 1905–2005: Tell Your Best Vegas Story*, http://www.lasvegas2005.org/interactive/lvstory77.htm.

Galbraith, James K. *Created Unequal: The Crisis in American Pay*. Chicago: University of Chicago Press, 2000.

Garcia, F. Chris, Christine Marie Sierra, and Margaret Maier Murdock. "The Politics of Women and Ethnic Minorities." In *Politics and Public Policy in Contemporary American West*, edited by Clive S. Thomas. Albuquerque: University of New Mexico Press, 1991.

Geran, Trish. *Beyond the Glimmering Light: The Pride and Perseverance of African Americans in Las Vegas*. Las Vegas: Stephens Press, 2006.

Goldwin, Robert A. "The U.S. Constitution Guarantees Social Justice." In *Social Justice: Opposing Viewpoint*, edited by Carol Wekesser and Karin Swisher. San Diego, Calif.: Greenhaven Press, 1990.

Goodrich, James. "Negroes Can't Win in Las Vegas," *Ebony*, Vol. 1 (1954).

Goodwin, Joanne. "Sarann Knight-Preddy," *Nevada Online Encyclopedia*, http://www.onlinenevada.org/sarann_knight_preddy,_entrepreneur.

Goodwin, Kristi. "Putting a New Face on the Past," *Las Vegas Style*, November 1992.

Green, Marian. "Moulin Rouge denied grant," *Las Vegas Review-Journal*, November 16, 1995.

_____. "Pequots eye Las Vegas," *Las Vegas Review-Journal*, April 19, 1996.

Green, Michael. "Backstory: Requiem for the Rouge," *Las Vegas Mercury*, June 5, 2003.

_____. "Moulin Rouge Hotel," *Nevada Online Encyclopedia*, http://www.onlinenevada.org/moulin_rouge.

Henry, Tamara. "School's Out for Assumptions: Many poor, minority students Out-Achieve Wealthy Districts," *USA Today*, December 13, 2001.

"The Historic Moulin Rouge Preservation Association, Inc."(Informational and donation flier), 1996.

"History of the Moulin Rouge — Then and Now," *38th Year Birthday Celebration*, collectors' edition (May 21, 22, 23, 1993).

Holland, Jearold Winston. *Black Recreation: A Historical Perspective*. Chicago: Burnham Inc., 2002.

Hooks, Doraine A. "Contributions of Black Theology." In *African American Sociology*, edited by James L. Conyers, Jr., and Alva P. Barnett. Chicago: Nelson-Hall Publishers 1999.

"Hotel Gets Drop in Property Tax," *Las Vegas Sun*, January 15, 1976.

"Hotel History: Moulin Rouge Hotel & Casino," *Las Vegas Now 71*, (Centennial, 2005).

Bibliography

"How Racism Affects the Mind—and Body," *The Wall Street Journal*, July 16, 2007.

Huey, Erik C. "Fitzgeralds owner upbeat on downtown," *Las Vegas Review-Journal*, February 20, 2004.

Hughes, Langston, Meltzer, Milton, Lincoln, C. Eric and Spencer, Jon Michael. *A Pictorial History of African Americans*, 6th rev. ed. New York: Crown Publishers, 1995.

Hulse, James W. *Forty Years in the Wilderness: Impressions of Nevada, 1940–1980.* Reno: University of Nevada Press, 1986.

_____. *The Silver State*, 2nd ed. Reno and Las Vegas: University of Nevada Press, 1998.

Hyman, Harold, and Bob Palm. "Black Las Vegans Forge Ahead Only to Fall Behind," *Las Vegas Sun* (1979).

_____. "Many Black Hotel Workers Charge Loss of Jobs Due to the Color of Their Skin," *Las Vegas Sun* (1979).

Illia, Tony. "Moulin Rouge makeover moves forward," *Business Press*, December 3, 2007.

"In This Era of Megamergers, Community Banks Thrive," *Las Vegas Review-Journal*, October 4, 1996.

Jenkins, Robin. "Moulin Rouge to Reopen," *Indian Voices*, January 1993.

Johns, Albert Cameron. *Nevada Politics*, 2nd ed. Dubuque, Iowa: Kendall/Hun Publishing, 1976.

Johnson, Lubertha, Jamie Coughtry, and R.T. King. *Lubertha Johnson: Civil Rights Efforts in Las Vegas: 1940–1960s.* Reno: University of Nevada Press Oral History Program, 1988.

Johnson, Ollie A., and Karin L. Stanford, eds. *Black Political Organizations in the Post-Civil Rights Era.* New Brunswick, N.J.: Rutgers University Press, 2002.

Kalil, J.M., and Frank Curreri. "ATF agents will investigate blaze at Moulin Rouge," reviewjournal.com-News.http://www. reviewjournal.com/lvrj_home/2003/May-30-Fri-2003/n... (1/15/2008, 1:53 PM).

Kaufman, Perry Bruce. "The Best City of Them All: A History of Las Vegas, 1930–1960." Ph.D. diss., University of California, Santa Barbara, 1974.

Kaus, Mickey. *The End of Equality.* New York: Basic Books, 1992.

Keleman, Matt. "Hidden Histories," *City Life*, December 9–15, 2004.

Kelly, Norman. *The Head Negro in Charge Syndrome: The Dead End of Black Politics.* New York: Nation Books, 2004.

Koch, Ed. "Blaze is latest chapter in hotel's storied history," *Las Vegas Sun*, May 29, 2003.

_____. "Breaking the rules when needed, he taught against prejudice," *Las Vegas Sun*, July 11, 2007.

_____. "Historic casino faces challenges," *Las Vegas Sun*, May 28, 2005.

Land, Barbara, and Myrick Land. *A Short History of Las Vegas*, 2nd ed. Reno: University of Nevada Press, 2004.

Lawson, Jen. "Some features of Moulin Rouge salvageable," *Las Vegas Sun*, June 5, 2003.

Laxalt, Robert. *Nevada: A Bicentennial History.* Reno and Las Vegas: University of Nevada, 1977.

Litwack, Leon F. *Trouble in Mind: Black Southerners in the Age of Jim Crow.* New York: Alfred A. Knopf, 1998.

Makenta, Nefretiti. "A View from West Las Vegas." In *The Real Las Vegas: Life Beyond the Strip,* ed. by David Littlejohn. New York: Oxford University Press, 1999.
Malveaux, Julianne. "The 'lucky' world of black men?" *USA Today*, March 14, 2008.
McKinnon, Shaun. "Boundaries of Race Tumble," *Las Vegas Review-Journal*, April 26, 1993.
McMillan, James B. *Fighting Back: A Life in the Struggle for Civil Rights.* Oral history interviews by Gary E. Elliott, narrative by R.T. King. Reno: University of Nevada Oral History Program, 1997.
Mills, Charles W. *Blackness Visible: Essays on Philosophy and Race.* Ithaca and London: Cornell University Press, 1998.
Minogue, Kenneth. *Politics.* New York: Oxford University Press, 1995.
"Minority Home Loans Up Sharply Across U.S.," *Las Vegas Review-Journal*, October 31, 1996.
Miranda, M L. *A History of Hispanics in Southern Nevada.* Reno: University of Nevada Press, 1997.
Moehring, Eugene. *Resort City in the Sunbelt, Las Vegas, 1930–2000.* Reno and Las Vegas: University of Nevada Press, 2000.
Moehring, Eugene P., and Michael S. Green. *Las Vegas: A Centennial History.* Reno and Las Vegas: University of Nevada Press, 2005.
Moore, Thomas. "Vegas is getting smarter, older," *Prime*, November 1996.
Motley, Constance Baker. *Equal Justice under Law, an Autobiography.* New York: Farrar, Straus and Giroux, 1998.
"Moulin Rouge Hotel," *Wikipedia, the free encyclopedia,* http://en.wikipedia.org/wiki/Moulin_Rouge_Hotel.
"Moulin Rouge Hotel & Casino." Flier, 1990.
"Moulin Rouge Hotel Awaits Reopening," *Las Vegas Sun*, March 8, 1977.
"Moulin Rouge Hotel History Book." http://www.lasvegashistorybooks.com/moulin.htm.
Moulin Rouge Offered to County as Hospital," *Las Vegas Sun*, January 10, 1968.
Myers, Jim. *Afraid of the Dark: What Whites and Blacks Need to Know About Each Other.* Chicago: Lawrence Hill Books, 2000.
Myrdal, Gunnar. *An American Dilemma: The Negro Problem and Modern Democracy*, vol. 11. New York: Pantheon Books, 1972.
Nasser, Haya El. "Las Vegas moving from a circus act to a regular city," *USA Today*, February 28, 2006.
Nelson, Jill. *Straight, No Chaser: How I Became a Grown-Up Black Woman.* New York: Penguin Books, 1997.
"New $2.5 billion mega-resort planned," *Nevada Contractor*, June 2007.
"The New Vegas," *Cigar Aficionado,* March/April 2006.
Odessky, Dick. "New lease on life for Moulin Rouge," *Las Vegas Sun*, January 5, 1977.
Orleck, Annelise. *Storming Caesars Palace: How Black Mothers Fought Their Own War on Poverty.* Boston: Beacon Press, 2005.
Padgett, Sonya. "Next step for civil rights," *Las Vegas Review-Journal*, January 20, 2008.
Page, Clarence. "Blacks left behind despite changes in nation since the civil rights era," *Las Vegas Sun*, July 29, 2007.

Bibliography

"Palms Casino Resort," *Wikipedia, the free encyclopedia*, http://en.wikipedia.org/wiki/Palms_Casino_Resort.

Patton, Natalie. "Clark County School Board, District C," *Las Vegas Review-Journal*, August 28, 1996.

Pratt, Timothy. "Again, a Plan for Renewal," *Las Vegas Sun*, February 25, 2008.

_____. "January cold snap claimed squatter," *Las Vegas Sun*, March 6, 2007.

_____. "Story changes squalor doesn't," *Las Vegas Sun*, April 6, 2007.

Raadschelders, Jos C.N. *Government: A Public Administration Perspective*. Armonk, New York: M. E. Sharpe, 2003.

"Race Spat to Board," *Las Vegas Review-Journal*, October 13, 1963.

"Racial Bias Meeting Held," *Las Vegas Sun*, October 14, 1963.

Radke, Jace, and Jen Lawson. "Fire ravages historic Moulin Rouge casino," *Las Vegas Sun*, May 29, 2003.

Ray, Clarence, Blue, Helen M. and Coughtry, Jamie. *Clarence Ray: Black Politics and Gaming in Las Vegas, 1920s–1980s*. Reno: University of Nevada Oral History Program, 1991.

Rothman, Hal. *Neon Metropolis: How Las Vegas Started the Twenty-First Century*. New York: Routledge, 2002.

Rusco, Elmer. "The Civil Rights Movement in Nevada," *Nevada Public Affairs Review*, No. 2 (1987).

_____. "Letter to the Editor," *Nevada Historical Society Quarterly*, September 21, 1991.

Sawyer, Grant. *Hang Tough! Grant Sawyer: an activist in the governor's mansion*. Narrative by R.T. King, interviews by Gary E. Elliott. Reno: University of Nevada Oral History Program, 1993.

Schumacher, Geoff. "North Las Vegas can't escape Sin City," *Las Vegas Review-Journal*, September 24, 2006.

_____. *Sun Sin & Suburbia: An Essential History of Modern Las Vegas*. Las Vegas: Stephen Press, 2004.

Schwartz, David McGrath. "Historic building unwrapped," *Las Vegas Review-Journal*, July 3, 2007.

Sebelius, Steve. "Moulin Rouge will get $3 mil. city loan," *Las Vegas Sun*, March 7, 1996.

"$775,000 Damage Suit Filed Against LV Hotel," *Las Vegas Sun*, February 7, 1968.

Shepard, Joan. "City Council Approves W.L. Economic Development Plans," *Las Vegas Sentinel Voice*, Volume 13, Issue 20 (September 10, 1992).

Sidel, Ruth. *Battling Bias: The Struggle for Identity and Community on College Campuses*. New York: Penguin Books, 1994.

Simpson, Jeff. "On how one troubled business was turned around — and why some might not be saved," *Las Vegas Sun*, March 9, 2008.

Sitkoff, Harvard. *A New Deal for Blacks: The Emergence of Civil Rights as a National Issue: Volume I: The Depression Decade*. New York: Oxford University Press, 1978.

Smith, Doug. "Agassi gives all of himself on, off tennis court," *USA Today*, August 31, 2001.

Smith, Hubble. "Moulin Rouge renovation in limbo," *Las Vegas Review-Journal*, July 10, 2004.

Smith, John. "Moulin Rouge finally succumbs to slow burn of felonious neglect," *Las Vegas Review-Journal*, June 1, 2003.

Spillman, Benjamin. "Backers pitch redevelopment of neglected Moulin Rouge," *Las Vegas Review-Journal*, February 26, 2008.

_____. "Moulin Rouge gets another go," *Las Vegas Review-Journal*, October 5, 2007.

_____. "Moulin Rouge taps Epic Gaming," *Las Vegas Review-Journal*, March 6, 2008.

Squires, Michael. "From Its Ashes: group buys historic site," review-journal.com-News. http://www.reviewjournal.com/lvrj_home/2004/Jan-29-Thu-2004/n. (1/15/2008).

_____. "Group buys historic site," *Las Vegas Review-Journal*, January 29, 2004.

_____. "Restoration planned for Moulin Rouge," *Las Vegas Review-Journal*, March 21, 2001.

Steel, Shelby. *White Guilt: How Blacks and Whites Together Destroyed the Promise of the Civil Rights Era*. New York: HarperCollins, 2006.

Tate, Katherine. *From Protest to Politics: The New Black Voters in American Elections*. New York: Russell Sage Foundation, 1993.

Taylor, Richard B. *Moulin Rouge—Hotel History*. Las Vegas: Beehive Press, 1995.

Thevenot, Garri Geer. "Ex-wife claims Moulin Rouge executive owes child support," *Las Vegas Review-Journal*, April 9, 2007.

Thompson, Gary. "Stupak looks at Moulin Rouge makeover," *Las Vegas Sun*, May 26, 1999.

Todd, Richard. "Las Vegas, 'Tis of Thee," *The Atlantic Monthly*, February 2001.

Tolson, Jay. "A History of Belief," *U.S. News & World Report*, November 26/December 3, 2007.

Trotter, Joe William, Jr., ed. *The Great Migration in Historical Perspective: New Dimensions of Race, Class, and Gender*. Indianapolis: Indiana University Press, 1991.

Warman, Donald. "Commission Hears Moulin Rouge Issue," *Las Vegas Review-Journal*, October 17, 1963.

"We Shall Overcome—Moulin Rouge," http://www.cr.nps.gov/nr/travel/civilrights/nv1.htm.

"Welcome to West Las Vegas," *Official Ethnic Destination & Visitors Guide, Las Vegas Convention and Visitors Authority* (2000 edition).

Werner, Larry. "Black Pride: Rich culture, history legacy of Southern Nevada black community," *Las Vegas Review-Journal*, February 7, 1983.

Wexler, Sanford. *The Civil Rights Movement: An Eyewitness History, Introduction by Julian Bond*. New York: Facts On File, Inc., 1993.

Whaley, Sean. "Group list endangered sites," *Las Vegas Review-Journal*, May 15, 2004.

White, Claytee D. "African American History in the West Vignette: The Moulin Rouge," *Vignette: The Moulin Rouge*, http://faculty.washington.edu/9taylor/aa.vignetttes/org_moulin_rouge, 12/16/2006.

Wilson, Mildred M. "Entertain Them ... But." In *Nevada Towns & Tales, Volume II—South*, ed. by Stanley W. Paher. Las Vegas: Nevada Publications, 1982.

Wilson, William J. "The Significance of Social and Racial Prisms." In *Through Different Eyes: Black and White Perspectives on American Race Relations*, ed. by Peter I. Rose, Stanley Rothman, and William J. Wilson. New York: Oxford University Press, 1973.

Wolman, Harold L., and Norman C. Thomas. "Black Interests, Black Groups, and Black Influence in the Federal Policy Process: The Cases of Housing and Education," *The Journal of Politics*, Vol. 32 (1970).
Wright, Frank. "The Late, Late Show," *Nevada*, May-June 1993.
"Writ Re-Opens License Fight on Hideaway," *Las Vegas Sun*, November 13, 1968.

Index

Index

Index

Index

Index

Index

Index

Index